Schema Therapy for Beginners

The Simple Guide to Understanding Your Patterns
and Healing Your Past

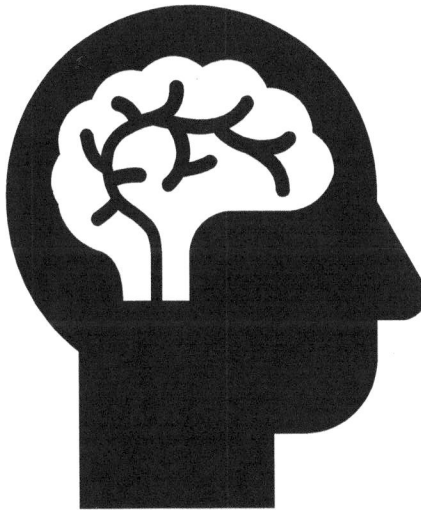

Kieran Tina Miles

ISBN: 978-1-7643835-7-8

First Edition: November 2025

This book is designed to provide information about schema therapy and psychological healing. It is sold with the understanding that the publisher and author are not engaged in rendering psychological, medical, or other professional services. If expert assistance or counseling is needed, the services of a competent professional should be sought.

The information provided in this book is based on research, clinical practice, and the author's understanding of schema therapy principles. However, every individual's situation is unique, and the techniques described may not be appropriate for everyone.

This book is not a substitute for professional mental health care. If you are experiencing severe depression, anxiety, suicidal thoughts, trauma, or other serious mental health concerns, please seek help from a qualified mental health professional immediately.

All names and identifying details of individuals mentioned in the examples throughout this book have been changed to protect privacy. Any resemblance to actual persons, living or dead, is purely coincidental. The case examples are composite illustrations based on common schema patterns and do not represent specific individuals.

The theories and techniques described are based on the work of Dr. Jeffrey Young and other schema therapy practitioners. This book represents the author's interpretation and presentation of these concepts for a general audience.

Crisis Resources:

If you are in crisis or having thoughts of suicide, please contact:

- **National Suicide Prevention Lifeline:** 988 (US)
- **Crisis Text Line:** Text HOME to 741741 (US)
- **International Association for Suicide Prevention:** https://www.iasp.info/resources/Crisis_Centres/

Medical Disclaimer: The information in this book is not intended to diagnose, treat, cure, or prevent any disease or medical condition. Always consult with a qualified healthcare provider before making any changes to your mental health treatment.

Table of Contents

About The Author 1

Preface...1

Chapter 1: What Is Schema Therapy....................................5

    The Day Everything Changed for Michael 5

    What Exactly Is Schema Therapy? 6

    Why Your Brain Keeps Running Old Programs...........7

    What Healing Actually Looks Like 8

    How to Use This Book..9

    You're Not Starting from Zero 9

Chapter 2: Your Core Emotional Needs..............................11

    The Five Core Emotional Needs 12

        The Interaction of Needs..18

        Your Needs Didn't Disappear 18

        Exercise: Identifying Your Unmet Needs 19

Chapter 3: The 18 Early Maladaptive Schemas...................22

    Domain 1: Disconnection and Rejection 22

    Domain 2: Impaired Autonomy and Performance 28

    Domain 3: Impaired Limits...32

    Domain 4: Other-Directedness.....................................34

    Domain 5: Overvigilance and Inhibition......................38

    Your Schema Profile 42

Chapter 4: Coping Styles..44

    The Three Coping Styles...44

        Coping Style #1: Surrender.....................................45

        Coping Style #2: Avoidance 47

Coping Style #3: Overcompensation 49

The Same Schema, Three Different Coping Styles 53

Mixing Coping Styles 53

Coping Styles in Relationships: The Dance...........................54

The Cost of Coping 55

Exercise: Identifying Your Coping Styles 55

From Coping to Healing 57

Chapter 5: Schema Modes 58

Why Modes Matter 58

The Four Categories of Modes...59

Child Modes: The Core of Your Emotions 59

Dysfunctional Coping Modes: Your Survival Strategies.........64

Dysfunctional Parent Modes: The Critical Voices..................67

Healthy Adult Mode: Your Goal 70

Tracking Your Modes 71

Mode Dialogues: Talking Between Parts.................................72

The Goal: Healthy Adult in Charge 74

Exercise: Meet Your Modes..75

Chapter 6: Schema Therapy Techniques..............................77

Cognitive Techniques: Working With Your Thoughts............77

Experiential Techniques: Working With Your Emotions........81

Behavioral Techniques: Working With Your Actions............85

Putting Techniques Together: A Complete Example..............88

Which Techniques Should You Use? 90

Important Reminders...90

Your Healing Plan...91

Chapter 7: Putting It All Together 93

Creating Your Personal Schema Map 93

Schema Work in Relationships 94

Schema Work at Work...99

Schema Work in Friendships 103

Schema Work in Parenting..104

Real-Life Transformations: Before and After.........................105

Your Action Plan for Real-Life Schema Work........................107

Common Challenges and How to Handle Them....................109

Final Encouragement 110

Chapter 8: Living Your New Story 112

Understanding That Schemas Don't Disappear....................112

The Stages of Schema Recovery...113

Building Resilience: Preventing Schema Relapses...............115

Deepening the Work: Advanced Schema Healing.................118

Teaching Schema Awareness to Your Children 120

The Ripple Effect: How Your Healing Helps Others 122

What Life Looks Like After Schema Work.............................122

Your New Story 124

The Practice of Maintenance...125

When to Seek Professional Help...126

Final Words: You're Not Done, and That's Okay 126

Resources for Your Continued Journey 128

Your Commitment 129

The End Is the Beginning...129

Appendix A: Schema Questionnaire for Self-Assessment........131

Appendix B: Schema Mode Inventory 140

Appendix C: Daily Schema Journal Template.........................146

Appendix D: Finding a Schema Therapist 155

Appendix E: Recommended Reading and Resources...............164

Glossary of Schema Therapy Terms 174

References 182

About The Author

As a registered mental health professional, I'm passionate about making psychological healing accessible to everyone, not just those who can decode clinical jargon. When I discovered schema therapy in my practice, I saw its transformative power firsthand—but I was frustrated by how difficult it was for everyday people to understand and apply this powerful approach to healing childhood wounds. Every resource seemed written for professionals, stuffed with terminology that regular people couldn't grasp.

So I created this comprehensive guide. Written in plain language with dozens of real-life examples, this book brings professional-level healing tools to anyone ready to break free from painful patterns. No confusing jargon. No complex theories. Just clear explanations and practical tools you can actually use.

I believe that understanding why you are the way you are is the first step to becoming who you want to be. And I believe that understanding shouldn't require a psychology degree—even though I have one.

Kieran Tina Miles, Registered Mental Health Professional

Preface

Let's Talk About Why You're Here

You know that thing you keep doing? The one you swore you'd never do again after the last time? The thing that makes you lie awake at 2am thinking, "Why am I like this?"

Yeah. That's why you're here.

Maybe it's picking the same type of wrong person over and over. Maybe it's working yourself into the ground while your inner voice screams that nothing you do is good enough. Maybe it's the way you agree to things you don't want to do, then spend the next week simmering with resentment. Or perhaps it's that special talent you have for sabotaging things right when they start going well.

Welcome to the club. Membership is surprisingly large.

The Thing Nobody Tells You

Here's what nobody mentions when you're struggling with these patterns: there's actually a reason you do what you do. A real, trackable, understandable reason. You're not just "messed up" or "self-destructive" or any of the other unhelpful labels people throw around.

You've got schemas.

Schemas are like software installed on your brain when you were a kid, designed to help you survive whatever your childhood threw at you. The problem is, you're now running thirty-year-old software on a completely different operating system, and it keeps crashing at the worst possible moments.

That's where schema therapy comes in. It's basically the instruction manual for understanding why you're still running that old programming—and how to update it.

Why I wrote this Book

I wrote this book because every other schema therapy resource I found read like it was written for people who already had three psychology degrees and a subscription to academic journals I'd never heard of. Lots of theory. Lots of jargon. Not a lot of "Oh, THAT'S why I do that thing with my relationships."

This book is different. It's written in actual human language. It has examples of real people (names changed, don't worry) doing real embarrassing things we've all done. It explains concepts without making you feel like you need a dictionary every three sentences.

Think of it as schema therapy translated from Academicese into something you'd actually say to a friend over coffee.

The Reality Check Section

Before we go further, let's get a few things straight:

This is not going to be easy. If you wanted easy, you'd have stuck with that book about positive affirmations and manifesting your dreams. This is real psychological work, which means it's sometimes uncomfortable, occasionally painful, and always worth it.

This is not fast. Sorry, but "Heal Your Childhood Wounds in Three Simple Steps" was already taken by books that don't work. Real change takes time—usually months or years, not days or weeks.

This might bring up feelings. You're going to recognize yourself in some unflattering ways. You might get sad, angry, or feel that creeping sense of "oh no, I've been doing this my whole life." That's actually a good sign. It means you're seeing clearly, probably for the first time.

You might need more help than a book. If you're dealing with serious trauma, active suicidal thoughts, severe depression, or other major mental health issues, please work with a therapist. This book can help, but it's not a replacement for professional care when that's what you need.

How This Thing Is Organized

The book follows a logical path (I know, shocking for a self-help book):

First, you'll learn what schemas are and where they come from. Then you'll figure out which ones you have—like a personality quiz, but less fun and more useful. Next, you'll understand how you've been trying to cope with them (spoiler: your coping methods are probably part of the problem). After that, we get into the actual healing work with real techniques you can use. Finally, we talk about applying all this to your actual life and keeping the changes going.

There are also appendices with assessment questionnaires, journaling templates, and resources—basically all the practical tools you need to actually do this work instead of just reading about it.

How to Actually Use This Book

Read Chapters 1-3 first. They're the foundation. Everything else builds on them. Skipping ahead is like trying to build the roof before the walls—technically possible, but not recommended.

Get a notebook. Not a "someday I'll write in this beautiful journal" notebook. An actual "I'm going to scribble insights at 11pm and maybe cry a little" notebook. You'll want to write things down as you go.

Do the exercises. I know, I know. Nobody wants to do exercises. But here's the thing: reading about your patterns is interesting. Working with them is what creates change. The exercises aren't busy work—they're where the magic happens. Or the hard work happens. Sometimes it's hard to tell the difference.

Take breaks when you need them. If a chapter hits particularly hard, put the book down. Take a walk. Call a friend. Watch something mindless on TV. This stuff can be heavy, and there's no prize for pushing through when you need a breather.

Come back to it. You're probably not going to read this once and be cured forever (if only). Schema work is ongoing. You'll likely need to revisit chapters as you grow and new patterns emerge.

What You're Actually Going to Get Out of This

If you stick with this—and I mean actually do the work, not just highlight things and feel vaguely inspired—here's what changes:

You'll start catching yourself mid-pattern and think, "Oh, there's my abandonment schema acting up" instead of spiraling into panic. You'll understand why you're attracted to people who are bad for you and actually start choosing differently. You'll recognize when your inner critic is being ridiculous and tell it to sit down. You'll set boundaries without feeling like a terrible person. You'll stop apologizing for existing.

And maybe, just maybe, you'll start feeling like you're living your actual life instead of repeatedly acting out scenes from childhood.

One Last Thing Before We Start

Look, I get it. Opening a book like this means admitting you've got work to do on yourself. That takes guts. It's way easier to just keep doing what you've always done and complaining about the results.

But you didn't pick the easy route. You picked this book, which means you're ready to understand why you are the way you are—and do something about it.

Your schemas have been running the show for long enough. They did their job when you were young. But you're not young anymore, and you don't need protection from things that aren't threatening you now.

It's time to take over.

Let's get started.

Kieran Tina Miles

Chapter 1: What Is Schema Therapy

Have you ever caught yourself thinking, "Why do I keep doing this?" Maybe you pick partners who treat you badly, even though you promise yourself you won't. Maybe you work yourself to exhaustion trying to be perfect, but nothing ever feels good enough. Maybe you push people away right when they start getting close, or perhaps you stay silent about your needs until you explode in anger.

If any of this sounds familiar, you're not broken. You're not weak. You're human, and you're running on old programming that made sense once but doesn't work anymore.

That's where schema therapy comes in.

The Day Everything Changed for Michael

Let me tell you about Michael, a 34-year-old accountant who came to therapy after his third relationship fell apart in almost the exact same way. Each time, things started well. He'd meet someone wonderful, fall in love, and feel happy. Then, a few months in, he'd start testing them. He'd cancel plans last minute. He'd pick fights over small things. He'd pull away emotionally, waiting—almost expecting—them to leave.

And they always did.

"I don't understand," Michael told his therapist during their first session. "I want a relationship. I really do. But it's like I'm watching myself destroy it, and I can't stop."

His therapist introduced him to schema therapy, and for the first time, Michael's behavior started to make sense. He wasn't sabotaging his relationships because he was crazy or self-destructive. He was following a pattern that formed when he was seven years old, after his mother left the family without warning. Young Michael learned a painful lesson: people you love will leave you. So adult Michael had developed a strategy—push them away first, before they can hurt you.

The pattern was protecting him from the pain he felt as a child. The problem? It was also preventing him from having the love he desperately wanted.

What Exactly Is Schema Therapy?

Schema therapy was developed in the 1990s by Dr. Jeffrey Young, a psychologist who worked with patients who weren't getting better with traditional therapy. These people understood their problems intellectually. They could talk about their childhoods and identify unhealthy patterns. But somehow, they couldn't change.

Young realized something important: knowing what's wrong isn't enough. You have to understand and heal the emotional wounds underneath.

Think of schemas as deep grooves in your mind, carved out by repeated childhood experiences. Once these grooves are there, your thoughts and feelings naturally flow down those same paths, even when you don't want them to. Schema therapy doesn't just help you understand these patterns—it helps you create new pathways.

Here's what makes schema therapy different from other approaches:

It focuses on your emotional needs. Regular therapy might help you identify negative thoughts. Schema therapy asks: what did you need as a child that you didn't get? Love? Safety? Freedom? Acceptance? And how can we help you get those needs met now?

It takes your past seriously. You're not dwelling on the past or using it as an excuse. You're understanding how your childhood experiences shaped the way you see yourself and the world. You can't change what happened, but you can change what you do with it.

It works with different parts of you. Sometimes you feel like a scared child. Sometimes you hear a harsh, critical voice in your head. Sometimes you shut down completely. Schema therapy helps you recognize these different "modes" (we'll talk more about these later) and teaches your healthy, adult self to take care of them.

It uses your emotions, not just your thoughts. You won't just talk about your problems. You'll do exercises that help you feel and process the emotions you've been avoiding.

Why Your Brain Keeps Running Old Programs

Here's something that helps explain why we get stuck in patterns: your brain learned most of its lessons about relationships and safety before you were old enough to think logically.

When you're a child, you don't have the ability to say, "My father's anger is about his own stress, not about me." Instead, you learn: "I must be bad. I need to be perfect to be safe."

These early lessons get stored deep in your nervous system. They become automatic. By the time you're an adult, you're reacting to situations based on what you learned at age five or eight or twelve—and you don't even realize it.

Jessica, a 29-year-old graphic designer, always felt anxious when her boss called her into his office. Even for good news—a promotion, a raise, a compliment on her work—her heart would race, her palms would sweat, and she'd spend the walk to his office mentally preparing to be fired.

This made no sense to Jessica. She was good at her job. She'd never been fired from anything. But her body remembered something her conscious mind had forgotten: when she was a child, being called into her father's study always meant punishment. Her nervous system learned: authority figure calls you = danger. That pattern was still running twenty years later.

What Healing Actually Looks Like

Let me be honest with you: schema therapy isn't a quick fix. You didn't develop these patterns overnight, and you won't heal them overnight either. But here's what you can expect:

You'll start recognizing your patterns. Instead of just feeling bad, you'll understand why you feel bad. You'll catch yourself mid-pattern and think, "Oh, that's my abandonment schema talking."

You'll learn where your patterns came from. You'll connect the dots between past experiences and present behavior. This isn't about blaming your parents or anyone else. It's about understanding.

You'll develop new ways of coping. Instead of avoiding, shutting down, or overreacting, you'll learn healthier responses. You'll build what schema therapy calls your "Healthy Adult" mode.

You'll get your needs met. Maybe for the first time, you'll learn to recognize what you actually need emotionally and find healthy ways to meet those needs.

Let me tell you what happened to Michael. After several months of schema therapy, he started dating again. When his girlfriend got busy with a work project and couldn't see him as much, Michael felt that familiar panic rising. But this time, instead of picking a fight or pulling away, he did something different.

He told her the truth: "I'm feeling scared right now. Part of me is worried you're going to disappear like my mother did. I know that's not logical, but that's what I'm feeling."

His girlfriend listened and reassured him. They made plans for the following week. The panic passed. The relationship continued. For the first time in his life, Michael didn't destroy something good because of his fear.

That's what healing looks like. Not perfect. Not pain-free. But different.

How to Use This Book

This book is designed to be practical. Each chapter will explain a concept and then show you what it looks like in real life. You'll meet people like you—people with jobs and families and problems—who learned to recognize and heal their schemas.

Here's what we'll cover:

- Your core emotional needs and what happens when they're not met
- The 18 common schemas that develop from childhood wounds
- The ways you've learned to cope with painful schemas (and why those strategies don't work)
- The different emotional "modes" you shift between during the day
- Specific techniques you can use to start healing

You can read this book cover to cover, or you can skip to the chapters that speak to you most. But I'd recommend reading Chapters 2 and 3 carefully, even if you want to skim the rest. Understanding your needs and identifying your specific schemas is the foundation for everything else.

Get a notebook. You'll want to write things down as you read. Memories will surface. Connections will form. Patterns will become clear. Write it all down.

Be patient with yourself. You're about to learn things about yourself that might be uncomfortable. You might remember painful experiences. You might see yourself in examples that are hard to look at. That's okay. That's actually good. It means you're doing the work.

You're Not Starting from Zero

Here's something important to remember: you've already survived. Whatever happened in your childhood, whatever patterns you developed, whatever pain you've carried—you made it through. The coping strategies that now cause problems once helped you survive difficult situations. They served a purpose.

Now you're ready to do more than survive. You're ready to heal and grow.

Carlos, a 42-year-old teacher, said something powerful in his first therapy session: "I spent the first half of my life becoming who I needed to be to survive. I want to spend the second half becoming who I actually am."

That's what this book is about. Not erasing who you are. Not pretending your past didn't happen. But understanding how you became you, appreciating the strength it took to get here, and choosing consciously how you want to move forward.

Your patterns make sense. Your reactions make sense. Your struggles make sense. And healing is possible.

Chapter 2: Your Core Emotional Needs

Every human being is born with the same basic needs. We need food and water and shelter, yes. But we also need something less tangible and just as important: we need to feel safe, loved, valued, and capable.

When these emotional needs are met consistently in childhood, we develop a healthy sense of self. We learn that we're worthy of love, that we can handle challenges, that we can trust others, and that the world is generally a safe place.

When these needs aren't met—or worse, when they're violated—we develop schemas. We create mental frameworks that help us make sense of painful experiences, and these frameworks stay with us into adulthood.

Let me give you an example. Emma grew up with a mother who was loving one day and cold the next, depending on her mood. Young Emma never knew which version of her mother she'd encounter. She learned to be constantly alert, reading her mother's face for danger signs, adjusting her behavior to avoid rejection.

Emma's emotional need for stable, consistent love wasn't met. So she developed a schema: people are unpredictable and will abandon you if you're not careful. As an adult, Emma was anxious in every relationship, constantly scanning for signs of rejection, interpreting every small action as potential abandonment.

The pattern made sense. It helped child-Emma survive an unpredictable home environment. But it was destroying adult-Emma's chance at healthy relationships.

The Five Core Emotional Needs

Dr. Young identified five categories of emotional needs that all children have. Let's look at each one and what happens when it's not met.

Need #1: Secure Attachments to Others

This is the big one. Children need to feel safe, protected, nurtured, and accepted. They need to know that someone will be there for them, consistently and reliably.

This includes several specific needs:

Safety and stability: Knowing that your home is secure, that adults will protect you, that your world isn't going to fall apart.

Nurturance: Receiving physical affection, emotional warmth, attention, and care.

Acceptance: Being loved for who you are, not for what you do or how you perform.

When these needs are met, children grow up feeling secure. They learn that relationships are safe, that people can be trusted, and that they're worthy of love.

When these needs aren't met, several schemas can develop. Let me show you what this looks like:

Marcus grew up in a chaotic home. His father had a drinking problem, and there were frequent late-night arguments. Sometimes his parents forgot to buy groceries. Sometimes the electricity got shut off because bills weren't paid. Young Marcus never felt safe. He couldn't rely on his parents to take care of basic needs.

As an adult, Marcus hoarded money obsessively. He had three months of expenses saved in cash under his mattress, even though he had a stable job and a good income. He checked his bank account multiple times a day. He couldn't relax on vacation because he was constantly worried about some disaster happening at home.

Marcus developed what's called a "vulnerability to harm" schema. He learned: the world is dangerous, and disaster could strike at any moment.

Diane had parents who provided everything materially but were emotionally cold. They never hugged her, rarely praised her, and seemed uncomfortable with emotions. When Diane was upset, they told her to "stop being dramatic" or "pull yourself together."

As an adult, Diane felt a deep loneliness, even when she was with people. She picked romantic partners who were emotionally unavailable, recreating the familiar feeling of wanting more than she could get. She couldn't identify her own emotions very well and felt empty inside.

Diane developed an "emotional deprivation" schema. She learned: no one will really be there for you emotionally. Don't expect nurturance or understanding.

Kevin was raised by a single mother who told him constantly that he was special, the most important person in her life, better than other kids. But underneath the praise, Kevin could feel that his mother needed him more than he needed her. She leaned on him emotionally, telling him adult problems, making him responsible for her happiness.

On the surface, it looked like Kevin's attachment needs were met—he was loved, even adored. But it was the wrong kind of love. His mother loved him for what he provided her, not for who he was.

As an adult, Kevin felt responsible for everyone's emotions. If his girlfriend was sad, it was his job to fix it. If a friend was disappointed, Kevin felt like he'd failed. He couldn't separate his feelings from others' feelings.

Kevin developed a "self-sacrifice" schema (we'll talk more about this later). He learned: your needs don't matter. Your job is to take care of others.

Need #2: Autonomy, Competence, and Sense of Identity

Children need to develop confidence in their ability to handle things on their own. They need to separate from their parents gradually, make age-appropriate decisions, and develop a sense of who they are as individuals.

When parents are overprotective, controlling, or don't allow children to try things and fail, this need goes unmet.

Rachel had well-meaning but anxious parents who did everything for her. They didn't let her walk to school alone, even in middle school. They called her teachers to handle any problems. They chose her classes, her activities, and her college major. They were always "helping," but the message Rachel received was: you can't handle things on your own.

As an adult, Rachel called her mother multiple times a day for advice on basic decisions. Should she buy this dress? Was she handling a work situation correctly? Was she sick or just tired? She felt paralyzed by simple choices and couldn't trust her own judgment.

Rachel developed a "dependence/incompetence" schema. She learned: I can't survive without help. I'm not capable of handling life on my own.

Antonio had the opposite problem. His parents were neglectful, leaving him to figure out everything himself from a young age. He made his own meals at seven, put himself to bed, and essentially raised himself. There was no guidance, no structure, no one teaching him how the world worked.

As an adult, Antonio struggled with basic self-discipline. He couldn't stick to a budget, showed up late to everything, left projects unfinished, and made impulsive decisions. He knew what he should do but couldn't seem to follow through.

Antonio developed an "insufficient self-control" schema. He learned: there are no boundaries or limits. I can do whatever I want, whenever I want.

Need #3: Freedom to Express Valid Needs and Emotions

Children need to learn that their feelings and needs are real, valid, and acceptable. They need permission to express emotions and have those emotions acknowledged.

When children are punished for expressing feelings, told that their needs don't matter, or made to feel that their emotions are wrong or too much, they learn to suppress their authentic selves.

Jennifer grew up in a family where anger was forbidden. Her parents never fought, never raised their voices, and expected Jennifer to be "good" at all times. When she got upset, they'd say things like, "We don't act like that in this family" or "Nice girls don't get angry."

As an adult, Jennifer couldn't express anger even when it was appropriate. When a coworker took credit for her work, she smiled and said nothing. When her partner forgot her birthday, she said it was fine. But the anger didn't disappear—it turned inward. Jennifer became depressed, developed stress-related health problems, and had explosive outbursts over tiny things because years of suppressed anger would suddenly break through.

Jennifer developed an "emotional inhibition" schema. She learned: feelings are dangerous. Keep them inside.

Ty had the opposite experience. His father had a violent temper, and Ty learned early that expressing any need or emotion could trigger an explosion. If he complained about being hungry, his father might yell at him for being ungrateful. If he cried, his father mocked him for being weak. If he got excited about something, his father would find a way to ruin it.

As an adult, Ty had trouble identifying what he wanted or needed. When friends asked where he wanted to eat, he'd say "I don't care" even when he did care. In relationships, he couldn't communicate his needs, which led to resentment and eventual breakup.

Ty developed a "subjugation" schema. He learned: expressing your needs leads to punishment. It's safer to have no needs at all.

Need #4: Spontaneity and Play

Children need to play, explore, be silly, make messes, and enjoy life. They need permission to be children, not miniature adults.

When parents are too serious, too strict, or give their children too much responsibility too early, this need goes unmet.

Linda was the oldest of five children in a family where both parents worked long hours. From age eight, Linda was responsible for her younger siblings. She made their meals, helped with homework, put them to bed. She had no time for friends, hobbies, or play. Her childhood was all duty and responsibility.

As an adult, Linda was a workaholic who couldn't relax. Vacations made her anxious. Hobbies felt like a waste of time. She felt guilty when she wasn't being productive. She couldn't understand why her children complained that she was "no fun."

Linda developed an "unrelenting standards" schema combined with self-sacrifice. She learned: life is serious business. Rest and play are for other people.

Nathan had parents who saw every activity as an opportunity for achievement. Sports weren't about fun—they were about winning. Hobbies needed to lead somewhere useful. Even play was structured and goal-oriented. There was no space for goofing around or doing things "just because."

As an adult, Nathan couldn't do anything without turning it into competition or achievement. He tracked every workout, turned cooking into a quest for perfection, and even played board games with his kids like they were Olympic events. He exhausted himself and everyone around him.

Nathan also developed an "unrelenting standards" schema. He learned: everything must have a purpose. Everything must be done perfectly.

Need #5: Realistic Limits and Self-Control

Children need boundaries. They need to learn that they can't always have what they want when they want it. They need to understand that actions have consequences and that other people's needs matter too.

When parents are too permissive, fail to set limits, or don't teach children to consider others, this need goes unmet.

Brandon was his parents' "miracle baby" after years of trying to conceive. They adored him and gave him everything he wanted. They never said no. They didn't enforce rules. When he got in trouble at school, they blamed the teachers. When he broke something, they bought a new one without consequences.

As an adult, Brandon struggled to keep jobs because he couldn't handle being told what to do. His relationships failed because he expected partners to cater to him constantly. He had massive credit card debt because he couldn't resist buying whatever he wanted.

Brandon developed an "entitlement/grandiosity" schema. He learned: rules don't apply to me. My needs are more important than others'.

Olivia had parents who were inconsistent with discipline. Sometimes they'd ignore bad behavior; other times they'd explode over small things. Olivia never knew what to expect, so she never learned clear boundaries.

As an adult, Olivia struggled with relationships because she didn't understand healthy boundaries. She'd overshare personal information immediately, get intensely involved in new friendships very quickly, and then feel hurt when people pulled back. She had trouble reading social cues and respecting others' limits.

Olivia didn't develop a specific "impaired limits" schema, but her lack of boundaries affected multiple areas of her life.

The Interaction of Needs

Here's something important to understand: these needs don't exist in isolation. Most people have unmet needs in multiple categories, and these interact with each other in complex ways.

Remember Michael from Chapter 1, whose mother left when he was seven? His need for secure attachment wasn't met (abandonment), which affected his ability to trust, which impacted his relationships, which prevented his need for emotional expression from being met (he couldn't be vulnerable), which reinforced his sense of isolation.

Think of unmet needs as creating a web of problems. One unmet need leads to behaviors that prevent other needs from being met, which creates more problems, which reinforces the original schema.

That's why schema therapy looks at the whole pattern, not just individual symptoms.

Your Needs Didn't Disappear

Here's the good news: even though your childhood needs weren't met back then, those needs didn't disappear. You still need security, autonomy, emotional expression, play, and healthy limits. You're still the same human with the same fundamental needs.

The problem is that your schemas—the patterns you developed to cope with unmet needs—now get in the way of getting those needs met in the present.

Think about it:

- If you learned you can't trust anyone (unmet attachment need), you probably push people away, which prevents you from getting the connection you crave.
- If you learned you're incompetent (unmet autonomy need), you probably depend on others excessively, which prevents you from developing confidence.
- If you learned your emotions are wrong (unmet expression need), you probably suppress feelings, which leads to depression or explosive anger.
- If you learned life is all work (unmet play need), you probably can't relax, which leads to burnout and resentment.
- If you learned you're special and rules don't apply (unmet limits need), you probably alienate people, which prevents you from having healthy relationships.

The patterns that once protected you now imprison you.

Exercise: Identifying Your Unmet Needs

Take some time with this. Get your notebook and write down your answers to these questions:

About Secure Attachment:

- Did you feel safe at home as a child?
- Were your parents emotionally available and warm?
- Could you count on adults to be there when you needed them?
- Were you accepted for who you were, or did you feel you had to earn love?
- Did you feel protected from harm?

About Autonomy and Competence:

- Were you encouraged to try new things and solve problems on your own?
- Did your parents let you make age-appropriate decisions?

- Did you develop a sense of who you were as an individual?
- Were you allowed to separate from your parents gradually?
- Did you feel capable and confident?

About Emotional Expression:

- Could you express all emotions in your family, or were some forbidden?
- Were your feelings acknowledged and validated?
- Did you feel heard and understood?
- Could you ask for what you needed?
- Was it safe to be vulnerable?

About Play and Spontaneity:

- Did you have time to just be a kid?
- Could you be silly and playful without criticism?
- Was life balanced between responsibility and fun?
- Were you allowed to explore interests without everything becoming about achievement?

About Limits and Self-Control:

- Were there clear, consistent rules and boundaries?
- Did you learn that actions have consequences?
- Were you taught to consider other people's feelings and needs?
- Did you learn healthy self-discipline?
- Did you understand that you couldn't always have what you wanted?

Don't rush through these questions. Your answers will help you understand which schemas you might have developed. There are no right or wrong answers—just honest ones.

You might notice emotions coming up as you answer. That's okay. That's part of the process. The child in you has been waiting a long time to be heard.

In the next chapter, we'll look at the specific schemas that develop when these needs go unmet. You'll learn their names, what they feel like, and how they show up in your adult life.

But for now, just sit with this awareness: your struggles aren't random. They're not character flaws. They're responses to unmet needs. And needs can be met, even now, even after all this time.

You're not too late.

Chapter 3: The 18 Early Maladaptive Schemas

- Your Life Patterns Explained

Now that you understand core emotional needs, let's look at what happens when those needs aren't met. This is where schemas come in.

Think of a schema as a lens through which you see the world. Once you develop a schema, you tend to notice evidence that confirms it and ignore evidence that contradicts it. If you have an abandonment schema, you'll interpret a partner's busy week as rejection. If you have a failure schema, you'll see a single mistake as proof you're incompetent. The schema acts as a filter, shaping what you see and how you interpret it.

Dr. Jeffrey Young identified 18 specific early maladaptive schemas. These schemas are organized into five domains based on which needs were unmet.

You probably won't have all 18 schemas. Most people have three to five strong schemas and maybe a few weaker ones. As you read through these, pay attention to which ones make your stomach clench or bring up emotions. Those are probably your schemas.

Let me introduce you to each one with real examples.

Domain 1: Disconnection and Rejection

These schemas develop when your need for secure, stable attachment wasn't met. People with schemas in this domain often feel different, isolated, or expect to be rejected or hurt by others.

Schema #1: Abandonment/Instability

The core belief: People close to me will leave. Relationships won't last. I'll end up alone.

What it looks like:

Remember Alex, whose father left the family when he was five? His dad promised to visit every weekend, but those visits became less frequent until they stopped altogether. Alex's mother struggled with depression after the divorce and was emotionally absent even when physically present.

As an adult, Alex was terrified of being left. In relationships, he was clingy and jealous. If his girlfriend didn't text back immediately, he'd panic and send multiple messages. If she made plans without him, he'd feel devastated. He'd constantly seek reassurance: "Do you still love me? You're not going to leave me, right?"

His partners initially found his attention flattering, but eventually they'd feel smothered. They'd pull back, which confirmed Alex's worst fear: see? Everyone leaves. He never saw that his behavior was pushing people away. His abandonment schema made sure he got abandoned, over and over.

Alex would also stay in bad relationships far too long because being treated poorly was better than being alone. His last relationship was with someone who was emotionally abusive, but Alex tolerated it for two years because leaving felt worse than staying.

Other signs of abandonment schema:

- Constant worry that your partner will leave
- Choosing people who aren't fully available (married people, people in other cities, people who explicitly say they don't want commitment)
- Overreacting to small signs of distance or unavailability
- Testing relationships to see if the person will stay
- Staying in unhealthy relationships because you can't tolerate being alone

Schema #2: Mistrust/Abuse

The core belief: People will hurt me, take advantage of me, manipulate me, or abuse me. I need to protect myself.

What it looks like:

Grace grew up with a father who was charming in public but cruel at home. He'd belittle her, mock her interests, and occasionally hit her. But to the outside world, he was a model parent. Grace learned early that you can't trust what people show you—underneath, they're probably dangerous.

As an adult, Grace assumed the worst about everyone's motives. If a coworker complimented her work, she wondered what they wanted. If someone was nice to her, she looked for the hidden agenda. When her boyfriend wanted to help her with a project, she accused him of trying to control her.

Grace kept people at arm's length. She shared nothing personal, never asked for help, and interpreted kindness as manipulation. She was hypervigilant, always watching for signs of danger. This exhausted her and kept her isolated.

Her mistrust was so strong that even when people treated her well, she couldn't let her guard down. She'd think, "They're just being nice now. Eventually they'll show their true colors." She collected evidence of small slights and overlooked genuine care.

Other signs of mistrust/abuse schema:

- Difficulty trusting anyone fully
- Assuming people have hidden, harmful motives
- Hypervigilance in relationships
- Testing people constantly
- Feeling safer alone than with others
- Reacting to small problems as if they're major betrayals
- Choosing relationships with people who confirm your belief that others will hurt you

Schema #3: Emotional Deprivation

The core belief: My emotional needs won't be met. No one will really understand me, care about my feelings, or give me the emotional support I need.

What it looks like:

There are actually three types of emotional deprivation:

Deprivation of nurturance: The belief that no one will take care of you physically or emotionally. Mitchell's parents were successful professionals who provided everything material but were emotionally distant. They didn't hug, didn't ask about his day, didn't comfort him when he was upset. As an adult, Mitchell couldn't ask for emotional support. When he was going through a hard time, he isolated himself rather than reaching out. He felt deeply lonely even in relationships.

Deprivation of empathy: The belief that no one will really listen to or understand you. Valerie's mother always dismissed her feelings: "You're being too sensitive. Stop making such a big deal out of nothing." As an adult, Valerie didn't share her feelings because she assumed no one would understand. She'd listen to friends' problems for hours but never talk about her own.

Deprivation of protection: The belief that no one will guide you or give you direction. James's parents were checked out, leaving him to figure out life on his own. As an adult, James felt adrift. He made decisions randomly because he never learned to trust his own judgment or ask for advice. He felt like a child playing at being an adult.

People with emotional deprivation schema often pick partners who are emotionally unavailable, recreating the familiar feeling of wanting more than they can get. They might also become the overfunctioning partner, giving endlessly while receiving little, because deep down they believe they don't deserve more.

Other signs of emotional deprivation schema:

- Feeling empty or alone even when with people
- Not asking for emotional support
- Choosing partners who are emotionally distant
- Giving much more than you receive in relationships
- Difficulty identifying your own emotional needs
- Feeling like no one really "gets" you

Schema #4: Defectiveness/Shame

The core belief: There's something fundamentally wrong with me. If people really knew me, they'd see how flawed I am and reject me.

What it looks like:

Patricia's mother was critical of everything. Her weight, her grades, her clothes, her friends, her personality—nothing was good enough. Her mother would make comments like, "If you just tried harder, you could be pretty" or "Why can't you be more like your sister?"

As an adult, Patricia felt like she was faking her way through life. She had a good job and friends, but she was convinced that if people saw the "real" her, they'd be disgusted. She hid parts of herself constantly. She never shared opinions that might be unpopular. She apologized excessively. She interpreted any criticism as confirmation that she was defective.

In relationships, Patricia sabotaged intimacy. When someone got close, she'd find a way to push them away before they could discover her "true" self. She had one-night stands but avoided real relationships. She'd think, "If they really knew me, they wouldn't want me."

The shame felt all-encompassing. It wasn't "I did something bad." It was "I am bad." Patricia couldn't separate her actions from her identity.

Other signs of defectiveness/shame schema:

- Feeling fundamentally flawed or damaged
- Hiding your "true self" from others
- Hypersensitivity to criticism
- Comparing yourself unfavorably to others
- Apologizing constantly
- Sabotaging relationships when someone gets too close
- Feeling like you're fooling people who think well of you

Schema #5: Social Isolation/Alienation

The core belief: I'm different from everyone else. I don't fit in. I don't belong anywhere.

What it looks like:

This schema is different from the others in this domain. It's less about expecting rejection and more about feeling fundamentally different, like you're on the outside looking in.

Roger grew up in a very religious community while his family wasn't religious. He felt different from the other kids, like he didn't understand the rules everyone seemed to know. His family was also lower-income in an affluent area, adding to his sense of not belonging.

As an adult, Roger always felt like an outsider. At parties, he'd stand on the sidelines, convinced he didn't fit in. At work, he'd eat lunch alone. He didn't join groups or activities because he assumed he wouldn't be welcome. He felt like everyone else got some manual for life that he never received.

The interesting thing about Roger's schema was that it was self-fulfilling. Because he felt different, he acted differently—standing apart, not engaging. This made people perceive him as aloof or uninterested, which reinforced his belief that he didn't belong.

Other signs of social isolation schema:

- Feeling like you don't fit in anywhere

- Believing you're fundamentally different from others
- Watching life from the outside
- Not joining groups or communities
- Feeling like everyone else understands social rules that you don't
- Isolating yourself because you assume you won't be accepted

Domain 2: Impaired Autonomy and Performance

These schemas develop when your need for autonomy, competence, and identity wasn't met. People with schemas in this domain often doubt their ability to function independently or to succeed.

Schema #6: Dependence/Incompetence

The core belief: I can't handle things on my own. I need someone else to help me make decisions and function in daily life.

What it looks like:

Lisa's mother was anxious and overprotective. She never let Lisa walk anywhere alone, choose her own clothes, or make any decisions. When Lisa got a B on a test, her mother called the teacher. When Lisa had a conflict with a friend, her mother intervened. The message was clear: you can't handle things yourself.

As an adult, Lisa called her mother multiple times a day for advice. "Should I accept this job offer? Is this a good apartment? Should I go to the doctor for this headache? Does this dress look okay?" She couldn't make decisions without reassurance.

Lisa also depended on romantic partners in unhealthy ways. She needed them to manage her finances, make social plans, and basically function as a parent. When relationships ended, she'd quickly find someone else to depend on because being alone felt terrifying.

The scary thing was that Lisa's incompetence was somewhat real—not because she couldn't learn, but because she'd never been allowed to practice. She'd developed a real skill deficit from years of dependence.

Other signs of dependence/incompetence schema:

- Constant need for reassurance and advice
- Difficulty making decisions alone
- Depending on others excessively for daily functioning
- Feeling helpless or overwhelmed by normal responsibilities
- Staying in relationships because you can't imagine managing alone
- Not developing skills because you assume you can't learn them

Schema #7: Vulnerability to Harm or Illness

The core belief: Catastrophe could strike at any time. I'm not safe. Something terrible is about to happen.

What it looks like:

Daniel's mother was a worrier who constantly predicted disasters. She'd tell him horror stories about plane crashes, kidnappings, diseases. She'd make him call her every few hours to "make sure he was okay." She'd rush him to the doctor for every minor symptom. Young Daniel learned: the world is dangerous.

As an adult, Daniel had severe health anxiety. Every headache was a brain tumor. Every chest pain was a heart attack. He Googled symptoms obsessively and visited doctors constantly. He had multiple health scares that turned out to be nothing, but each time he was convinced this was it—the catastrophe he'd always feared.

Daniel also worried about other disasters. He checked that his doors were locked multiple times. He wouldn't fly because of plane crash fears. He had extensive emergency supplies. He imagined worst-case scenarios constantly.

His anxiety was exhausting. He couldn't enjoy anything because he was always waiting for disaster. Vacations were ruined by worry. Good news was contaminated by fear of "the other shoe dropping."

Other signs of vulnerability schema:

- Excessive worry about health issues
- Catastrophic thinking (always imagining worst-case scenarios)
- Avoiding situations you perceive as dangerous
- Constant checking behaviors (locks, stoves, etc.)
- Inability to relax because you're waiting for disaster
- Hypervigilance about potential threats

Schema #8: Enmeshment/Undeveloped Self

The core belief: I don't have a clear identity separate from my parent/partner. I can't survive without being extremely close to them. I don't know who I am on my own.

What it looks like:

Christina's mother was overbearing and intrusive. She read Christina's diary, listened to her phone calls, and demanded to know every detail of her life. But she framed it as closeness: "We're best friends! We tell each other everything!" Christina's mother also shared inappropriate adult problems with her, treating her like a therapist.

As an adult, Christina still talked to her mother multiple times a day. She couldn't make decisions without discussing them with her mother first. She'd never developed her own opinions, interests, or identity—she just absorbed her mother's preferences. When someone asked Christina what she liked or wanted, she'd go blank. She didn't know.

In romantic relationships, Christina did the same thing. She'd lose herself completely in the relationship, adopting her partner's interests and opinions. When relationships ended, she felt like she disappeared because she had no separate self to fall back on.

The enmeshment felt suffocating but also necessary. Christina couldn't imagine being separate because she'd never developed the skills or identity to function independently.

Other signs of enmeshment schema:

- Excessive involvement with a parent or partner
- Difficulty making decisions without checking with someone else
- Not knowing your own preferences, opinions, or identity
- Feeling like you can't function without being extremely close to someone
- Absorbing others' emotions and opinions as if they're your own
- Guilt when trying to separate or be independent
- Feeling empty when alone

Schema #9: Failure

The core belief: I'm inadequate. I'll fail at anything important. I'm less capable than others.

What it looks like:

Jake's father constantly compared him unfavorably to his older brother. "Why can't you be smart like your brother? Why can't you play sports like your brother?" Nothing Jake did was good enough. His father predicted he'd never amount to anything.

As an adult, Jake felt like a failure even though objectively he was doing okay. He had a decent job, but he was convinced he was terrible at it and would be fired any day. He avoided challenges because failure felt inevitable. When he was offered a promotion, he turned it down because he was sure he couldn't handle it.

Jake compared himself to others constantly and always came up short. He focused on his failures and discounted his successes. When he did well at something, he attributed it to luck or outside help—never his own ability.

The failure schema was self-perpetuating. Because Jake believed he'd fail, he avoided opportunities and didn't try his best. This led to mediocre results, which confirmed his belief that he was inadequate.

Other signs of failure schema:

- Believing you're less competent than others
- Avoiding challenges because you expect to fail
- Focusing on your failures and discounting successes
- Comparing yourself unfavorably to others
- Not pursuing goals because you assume you can't achieve them
- Attributing success to luck rather than ability
- Underperforming because you've already given up

Domain 3: Impaired Limits

These schemas develop when your need for realistic limits and self-control wasn't met. People with schemas in this domain often struggle with self-discipline, respecting others' boundaries, or accepting that they can't always have what they want.

Schema #10: Entitlement/Grandiosity

The core belief: I'm special. The normal rules don't apply to me. My needs are more important than others'. I should get what I want.

What it looks like:

Trevor was his parents' golden child. They praised him constantly, told him he was smarter and better than other kids, and never enforced consequences. When he got in trouble, they blamed others. When he wanted something, they bought it. Trevor learned: I'm special, and I deserve whatever I want.

As an adult, Trevor was difficult to work with. He expected special treatment, cut in line, ignored rules he found inconvenient, and became angry when things didn't go his way. He had a string of failed relationships because he expected partners to cater to him without reciprocating.

Trevor genuinely couldn't understand why people found him arrogant. He thought, "I'm just being confident. Why are people so sensitive?" He didn't see that his behavior was self-centered and disrespectful.

The entitlement protected Trevor from feeling inadequate, but it prevented him from having genuine connections or achieving real success. People didn't want to work with him, and his relationships were shallow.

Other signs of entitlement schema:

- Believing rules don't apply to you
- Expecting special treatment
- Difficulty taking others' perspectives
- Rage when you don't get what you want
- Manipulating to get your way
- Lack of empathy for others' needs
- Arrogant or superior attitude
- Difficulty accepting criticism or consequences

Schema #11: Insufficient Self-Control/Self-Discipline

The core belief: I can't control my impulses. I should be able to do whatever I want, whenever I want. Self-discipline is too hard.

What it looks like:

Nicole's parents never enforced rules or consequences. If she didn't want to do homework, fine. If she wanted to eat ice cream for dinner, okay. If she threw tantrums, they gave in. Nicole learned that immediate gratification was more important than long-term goals and that she didn't need to control her impulses.

As an adult, Nicole struggled with everything requiring self-discipline. She couldn't stick to a budget and had massive credit card debt. She started projects but never finished them. She made impulsive decisions—quitting jobs without another lined up, buying things she couldn't afford, ending relationships over minor conflicts.

Nicole knew her behavior caused problems, but in the moment, she couldn't resist. She'd think, "I'll start my diet tomorrow. I deserve this donut today." Or "I know I should save money, but this dress is on sale and I want it now."

Her life felt chaotic and out of control. She'd resolve to change, maybe even stick with new habits for a few days, but then she'd slip back into old patterns.

Other signs of insufficient self-control schema:

- Difficulty delaying gratification
- Impulsive decisions
- Starting projects but not finishing them
- Inability to stick to budgets, diets, or other goals
- Choosing immediate pleasure over long-term benefits
- Difficulty with boring or routine tasks
- Giving up quickly when things get hard
- Outbursts of temper or emotion

Domain 4: Other-Directedness

These schemas develop when you learned that your needs don't matter as much as others' needs. People with schemas in this domain focus excessively on gaining approval, taking care of others, or suppressing their own desires.

Schema #12: Subjugation

The core belief: I have to give in to others' wishes or they'll punish me, abandon me, or retaliate. My needs and feelings don't matter.

What it looks like:

Maya grew up with an aggressive father who demanded obedience. If she expressed an opinion he didn't like, he'd yell or give her the silent treatment. If she didn't do exactly what he wanted, he'd make her feel guilty. Maya learned: expressing your needs is dangerous. It's safer to submit.

As an adult, Maya couldn't say no to anyone. Her coworkers dumped extra work on her because they knew she wouldn't refuse. Her friends made all the decisions because Maya never expressed preferences. In relationships, she went along with whatever her partner wanted, even when she was unhappy.

The frustrating thing was that Maya often didn't even know what she wanted. She'd suppressed her needs for so long that she'd lost touch with them. When someone asked, "What do you want for dinner?" she'd go blank.

Eventually, the suppressed resentment would build up. Maya would suddenly explode over something small, shocking everyone because she seemed so agreeable. Or she'd passive-aggressively sabotage things. But she could never directly assert her needs.

Other signs of subjugation schema:

- Difficulty saying no
- Suppressing your own feelings and needs
- Going along with others even when you disagree
- Feeling controlled by others
- Difficulty knowing what you want
- Building up resentment that explodes unexpectedly
- Avoiding conflict at all costs
- Guilt when you do express needs

Schema #13: Self-Sacrifice

The core belief: I must put others' needs first. Taking care of myself is selfish. My purpose is to help others.

What it looks like:

Self-sacrifice looks similar to subjugation, but the motivation is different. Subjugation comes from fear—fear of punishment or abandonment. Self-sacrifice comes from guilt and excessive responsibility.

Henry grew up with a sick mother who needed a lot of care. From a young age, Henry helped with her medical care, household tasks, and emotional support. He learned that his job was to take care of others, and his mother praised him for being "so helpful" and "such a good boy."

As an adult, Henry was everyone's go-to helper. He'd drop everything to help a friend move, stay late at work to cover for coworkers, and give money to family members who were irresponsible with finances. His own needs always came last.

Henry felt good about helping at first—it gave him purpose and made him feel needed. But over time, he felt drained and resentful. He couldn't understand why people didn't reciprocate. When he finally tried to set boundaries, he felt crushing guilt.

The difference between self-sacrifice and healthy generosity is that self-sacrifice is compulsive. Henry couldn't stop helping even when it hurt him. He felt responsible for everyone's happiness and wellbeing.

Other signs of self-sacrifice schema:

- Compulsively taking care of others
- Guilt when you prioritize your own needs
- Feeling responsible for others' happiness
- Difficulty receiving help
- Resentment that builds over time
- Feeling drained and burnout
- Choosing helping professions and overdoing it
- Martyrdom ("Look at everything I do for you")

Schema #14: Approval-Seeking/Recognition-Seeking

The core belief: I need approval, attention, and recognition from others to feel worthwhile. My value depends on what others think of me.

What it looks like:

Bethany's parents gave attention based on achievement. They praised her when she got good grades, won awards, or impressed others. But when she just wanted to hang out or needed comfort, they were distant. Bethany learned: my worth depends on impressing others.

As an adult, Bethany was obsessed with her image. She posted constantly on social media, checking compulsively for likes and comments. She chose jobs, activities, and even relationships based on how they looked to others, not what she actually wanted. She bought expensive things she couldn't afford because she wanted to appear successful.

Bethany was extremely sensitive to criticism or disapproval. If someone didn't seem impressed with her, she felt worthless. She'd go to great lengths to get validation—staying in the spotlight, bragging about achievements, or doing outrageous things for attention.

The exhausting part was that the approval never lasted. Each compliment or like gave her a brief boost, but then she needed more. She was like a person dying of thirst, drinking salt water—the more she got, the thirstier she became.

Other signs of approval-seeking schema:

- Basing decisions on others' opinions
- Obsessive focus on image and status
- Extreme sensitivity to criticism
- Need for constant validation and attention
- Choosing relationships and activities based on how they look
- Bragging or showing off
- Feeling worthless when you don't get recognition

- Comparing yourself to others constantly

Domain 5: Overvigilance and Inhibition

These schemas develop when you learned that you must be perfect, suppress emotions, or expect the worst. People with schemas in this domain are often rigid, pessimistic, or harsh with themselves and others.

Schema #15: Negativity/Pessimism

The core belief: Something bad will happen. Things will go wrong. Why focus on the positive when it won't last?

What it looks like:

Ellen grew up with parents who constantly worried and predicted bad outcomes. They'd say things like, "Don't get your hopes up—you'll just be disappointed" or "That's nice, but what could go wrong?" Ellen learned to expect the worst.

As an adult, Ellen couldn't enjoy good things. When she got a promotion, she immediately worried about increased expectations and potential failure. When she met someone nice, she focused on how it would eventually end. When planning a vacation, she obsessed about everything that could go wrong.

Ellen's negativity was self-protective. If you expect the worst, you won't be disappointed. But it robbed her of joy and optimism. She couldn't celebrate successes or feel hopeful about the future.

Her negativity also affected relationships. Ellen's pessimism was exhausting for others. When friends shared good news, she'd point out potential problems. When her partner suggested plans, she'd list reasons they wouldn't work out.

Other signs of negativity schema:

- Automatically expecting negative outcomes

- Focusing on problems rather than solutions
- Difficulty enjoying positive experiences
- "Yes, but..." responses to good news
- Preparing for disaster constantly
- Difficulty feeling hopeful or optimistic
- Minimizing positive aspects of situations
- Expecting disappointment

Schema #16: Emotional Inhibition

The core belief: I must control my emotions. Showing feelings is weak, embarrassing, or dangerous. I need to keep emotions inside.

What it looks like:

Robert grew up in a family where emotions were seen as weakness. His father would say, "Stop crying or I'll give you something to cry about" or "Man up." Showing vulnerability meant being mocked. Robert learned to shut down his emotions completely.

As an adult, Robert was extremely uncomfortable with feelings—his own and others'. When his wife cried, he'd leave the room or tell her to "calm down." When he felt sad or scared, he'd suppress it or channel it into anger (the one emotion that felt acceptable).

Robert appeared stoic and in control, but inside he felt disconnected from himself. He had stress-related health problems—headaches, digestive issues, high blood pressure—because his body was expressing the emotions he wouldn't allow himself to feel.

In relationships, Robert's emotional inhibition created distance. His wife felt lonely because he couldn't be vulnerable. His children learned to hide their feelings from him. He wanted connection but didn't know how to achieve it.

Other signs of emotional inhibition schema:

- Difficulty expressing emotions
- Discomfort when others show feelings

- Physical symptoms from suppressed emotions
- Belief that emotions are weak or dangerous
- Appearing stoic or shut down
- Channeling all emotions into anger or none at all
- Difficulty with intimacy
- Using humor or sarcasm to avoid genuine feeling

Schema #17: Unrelenting Standards/Hypercriticalness

The core belief: I must meet extremely high standards. Good enough isn't good enough. I must be perfect.

What it looks like:

Angela's parents had impossible expectations. Nothing she did was ever quite good enough. An A-minus wasn't celebrated—it was questioned: "Why not an A-plus?" When she won second place in a competition, they asked why she didn't win first. Angela learned that approval came only through perfection.

As an adult, Angela was a perfectionist who drove herself relentlessly. She worked long hours, couldn't delegate because others wouldn't do things "right," and beat herself up over tiny mistakes. She had impossibly high standards for herself and others.

Angela's perfectionism came at a cost. She was exhausted, anxious, and never felt satisfied. She couldn't enjoy accomplishments because she immediately focused on what could be better. Her relationships suffered because she was critical of partners and couldn't accept their imperfections.

The worst part was the internal critic. Angela's inner voice was harsh and unforgiving, constantly pointing out flaws and demanding more. Even when others praised her, she dismissed it because she knew all her shortcomings.

Other signs of unrelenting standards schema:

- Perfectionism that's never satisfied

- Extremely high standards for yourself and others
- Difficulty delegating or trusting others to do things
- Harsh self-criticism
- Never feeling good enough
- Difficulty relaxing or having fun
- Measuring worth by achievement and productivity
- Critical of others' mistakes
- Difficulty accepting "good enough"

Schema #18: Punitiveness

The core belief: People (including me) should be harshly punished for mistakes. There's no room for error. Forgiveness is weakness.

What it looks like:

Victor's father believed in harsh discipline. Small mistakes resulted in severe punishment—yelling, harsh criticism, or physical punishment. There was no understanding, no mercy, no second chances. Victor learned that mistakes deserve punishment and that people (including himself) need to be punished to learn.

As an adult, Victor was extremely hard on himself. When he made mistakes, he'd berate himself cruelly: "You're such an idiot. How could you be so stupid?" He'd punish himself—refusing to eat, working extra hours, or ruminating for days.

He was also harsh with others. When people made mistakes, Victor thought they deserved to suffer. He had no compassion, no understanding of human imperfection. He believed in retribution and justice, not forgiveness and growth.

Victor's punitiveness isolated him. People felt judged and unsafe around him. His children were afraid of him. His relationships lacked warmth because he couldn't forgive normal human failings.

Other signs of punitiveness schema:

- Harsh self-criticism and self-punishment

- Belief that people should suffer for mistakes
- Difficulty forgiving yourself or others
- Black-and-white thinking about right and wrong
- Rage at people who break rules or make errors
- Lack of compassion for human imperfection
- Using guilt, shame, or punishment to motivate self or others
- Difficulty with mercy or understanding

Your Schema Profile

Now that you've read about all 18 schemas, which ones resonated with you? Most people have three to five primary schemas with maybe a few secondary ones.

Get your notebook and write down:

- Which schemas felt immediately familiar?
- Which examples reminded you of yourself?
- Which schemas brought up emotions as you read?
- Which ones explain patterns in your life?

Don't worry if you identified with multiple schemas. They often work together. For example, someone might have abandonment, defectiveness, and subjugation schemas all interacting. The abandonment makes you fear people leaving, the defectiveness makes you feel unworthy of love, and the subjugation makes you suppress your needs to try to keep people around.

Remember, schemas aren't all-or-nothing. You might have a mild version of one schema and a severe version of another. You might also notice that schemas are stronger in certain situations or with certain people. That's normal.

The important thing is that you're starting to see the patterns. You're connecting the dots between your childhood experiences, the beliefs you formed, and the difficulties you face now.

In the next chapter, we'll look at how you've learned to cope with these painful schemas—and why those coping strategies, while understandable, often make things worse.

You're doing important work here. Stay with it.

Chapter 4: Coping Styles

Now you know about schemas—those deep patterns that formed in response to childhood experiences. But here's the thing: schemas are painful. They make you feel vulnerable, abandoned, defective, trapped, or inadequate. These feelings are unbearable, especially for a child.

So your brilliant, resourceful mind figured out ways to cope with schema pain. You developed strategies to protect yourself from these uncomfortable feelings. These coping strategies helped you survive difficult circumstances. They made sense at the time.

The problem? The same coping strategies that once protected you now trap you. They prevent you from healing your schemas and getting your needs met. They keep you stuck in the very patterns you want to escape.

Let's look at the three main coping styles and how they show up in real life.

The Three Coping Styles

Dr. Young identified three basic ways people cope with schemas: surrender, avoidance, and overcompensation. Most people use different coping styles for different schemas, though you might have one style that's your "go-to" response.

Think of these as fight, flight, and freeze responses to emotional pain:

- **Surrender** = freeze (give in to the schema)
- **Avoidance** = flight (run away from schema triggers)
- **Overcompensation** = fight (do the opposite of what the schema predicts)

None of these are wrong or bad. They're strategies your mind created to help you survive. But as we'll see, they all end up reinforcing the very schemas you're trying to escape.

Coping Style #1: Surrender

When you surrender to a schema, you accept it as true. You give up fighting it and behave in ways that confirm the schema's predictions. It's like saying, "I guess this is just how I am" or "This is what I deserve."

Surrender feels like resignation or acceptance, but it's actually a protective strategy. If you accept that the schema is true, you don't have to keep hoping for something different. You don't have to risk disappointment or fight against reality.

Let me show you what surrender looks like with different schemas:

Surrender + Abandonment Schema

Remember Alex from Chapter 3, who was terrified people would leave him? In his early twenties, Alex tried a different approach. Instead of being clingy, he just...accepted that people would leave.

He'd start relationships already knowing they'd end. He'd think, "Might as well enjoy it while it lasts." He'd do nothing to maintain the relationship—wouldn't plan dates, wouldn't work through conflicts, wouldn't invest emotionally. When the relationship inevitably ended, he'd shrug and say, "See? I knew it. Everyone leaves."

Alex was surrendering to his abandonment schema. By not investing, he protected himself from the pain of loss. But his surrender behavior—the distance, the lack of effort—actually caused relationships to fail. His schema created a self-fulfilling prophecy.

Surrender + Defectiveness Schema

Camille believed she was fundamentally flawed. In high school and college, she fought against this belief, trying to prove she was worthwhile. But eventually, she got tired of fighting.

She surrendered. She stopped trying to connect with people. She took jobs below her capability because "someone like me doesn't deserve better." She dated people who treated her poorly because "that's what I deserve." When good opportunities came up, she didn't pursue them because "people like me don't get chances like that."

Camille's surrender protected her from disappointment and rejection. If she didn't try, she couldn't fail. If she accepted her "defectiveness," she didn't have to feel the pain of trying and being rejected. But her surrender prevented her from discovering that her schema was wrong.

Surrender + Subjugation Schema

Remember Maya, who couldn't say no to anyone? She surrendered completely to her subjugation schema. She accepted that her needs didn't matter and that her role was to please others.

She'd automatically say yes to requests without even checking if she wanted to. She'd go along with others' plans without considering her preferences. She'd stay in relationships where she was mistreated because "that's just how relationships are."

Maya's surrender prevented conflict and punishment. By never asserting herself, she stayed "safe." But her surrender meant her needs never got met, and she built up massive resentment that had no healthy outlet.

Why Surrender Keeps You Stuck:

When you surrender to a schema, you never test whether it's actually true. You never have experiences that could contradict the schema. You're so busy confirming it that you can't see evidence against it.

If Alex had invested in relationships, maybe some would have lasted. If Camille had pursued opportunities, maybe she'd have discovered her competence. If Maya had expressed her needs, maybe some people would have respected them.

But surrender prevents these healing experiences from happening.

Coping Style #2: Avoidance

When you avoid a schema, you do everything possible not to feel the schema pain. You stay away from situations that might trigger the schema. You numb your emotions. You distract yourself. You shut down.

Avoidance can be obvious—like avoiding relationships if you have an abandonment schema. But it can also be subtle—like staying busy to avoid feeling lonely, or drinking to numb painful emotions.

Avoidance feels like safety. If you don't get close to people, they can't abandon you. If you don't try challenging things, you can't fail. If you don't feel your emotions, they can't hurt you. But avoidance keeps you stuck because you never work through the painful feelings or learn that you can survive them.

Avoidance + Abandonment Schema

Spencer had a severe abandonment schema after his mother died when he was nine. As an adult, Spencer avoided relationships completely. He'd go on a few dates, feel himself getting attached, and then disappear. He'd make excuses—too busy with work, not ready for a relationship, the timing was wrong.

Spencer also had a version called the "Detached Protector" mode. He'd shut down his emotions completely. He felt numb most of the time, disconnected from people. He spent his evenings watching TV or gaming—anything to avoid the lonely feelings underneath.

Spencer's avoidance protected him from the terror of loss. If he never got attached, he couldn't be abandoned. But his avoidance also meant he lived a lonely, isolated life. The very thing he feared—being alone—was what his avoidance created.

Avoidance + Failure Schema

Paula believed she would fail at anything important. Her avoidance looked like procrastination and underachievement. She'd sign up for classes but drop them before the first test. She'd apply for jobs below her qualifications. She'd start projects but never finish them.

Paula kept herself safe by never really trying. If you don't try, you can't fail, right? She could tell herself, "I didn't fail—I just didn't try." But her avoidance meant she never achieved anything, which reinforced her belief that she was inadequate.

Paula also avoided feedback. She didn't ask for performance reviews at work. She didn't show people her creative projects. She avoided any situation where she might be evaluated or judged. This protected her from confirmation of her failure schema, but it also prevented her from getting positive feedback that might challenge it.

Avoidance + Defectiveness Schema

Brandon felt deeply ashamed of who he was. His avoidance looked like hiding. He didn't share personal information. He kept conversations superficial. He had lots of acquaintances but no close friends. He avoided intimacy in relationships.

Brandon also used substances to avoid feeling his shame. Drinking or smoking weed numbed the painful feelings. It gave him temporary relief from the constant voice in his head saying he was defective and unworthy.

Brandon's avoidance kept him safe from rejection—no one could reject the real him because no one knew the real him. But it also meant he lived behind a wall, unable to experience genuine connection or love.

Different Forms of Avoidance

Avoidance can look many different ways:

- **Physical avoidance:** Staying away from triggering situations
- **Emotional avoidance:** Shutting down feelings or staying numb
- **Cognitive avoidance:** Not thinking about painful topics, staying distracted
- **Substance use:** Alcohol, drugs, food, or other substances to numb pain
- **Activity avoidance:** Staying constantly busy to avoid facing feelings
- **Social avoidance:** Isolating, not forming close relationships
- **Selective memory:** "Forgetting" painful events or feelings

Why Avoidance Keeps You Stuck:

Avoidance prevents you from facing and working through painful emotions. You never learn that you can survive schema feelings. You never test whether your schema predictions are true. You never have corrective experiences that could heal the schema.

Avoidance also has side effects. Numbing pain means numbing joy too. Avoiding relationships means missing connection. Staying safe means missing life.

And here's the hardest part: the thing you're avoiding—the feared outcome—often happens anyway because of the avoidance itself. Spencer avoided relationships to prevent abandonment, but he ended up alone. Paula avoided challenges to prevent failure, but she ended up underachieving. Brandon avoided intimacy to prevent rejection, but he ended up isolated.

Coping Style #3: Overcompensation

When you overcompensate for a schema, you do the opposite of what the schema predicts. You fight against it. You try to prove the schema wrong through your behavior.

Overcompensation can look like strength or confidence on the outside. But inside, it's driven by fear and pain. You're not acting from a place of genuine health—you're reacting against the schema.

Think of overcompensation as the mind saying, "I'll never let that happen to me again." It's a protective rebellion against schema pain.

Overcompensation + Abandonment Schema

Tyler had severe abandonment fears, but unlike Alex, he didn't become clingy. He overcompensated by being the one who left first. He'd end relationships at the first sign of trouble. If someone got too close, he'd push them away. If he sensed any distance, he'd bolt.

Tyler told himself he was independent and didn't need anyone. He'd say, "I'm fine alone. Relationships are too much work." But underneath, he was terrified of being left. His overcompensation—leaving first—was a pre-emptive strike against abandonment.

Tyler also overcompensated by being in control. He had to make all the decisions, plan everything, maintain emotional distance. If he was in control, he reasoned, he couldn't be abandoned. But his controlling behavior pushed people away, creating the very outcome he feared.

Overcompensation + Defectiveness Schema

Isabella felt deeply defective and flawed. Her overcompensation looked like perfectionism and overachievement. She got straight A's, advanced quickly in her career, maintained a perfect appearance. She presented an image of confidence and competence.

But underneath, Isabella was driven by the terror that people would see the "truth" about her. She had to be perfect because if she wasn't, people would see she was defective. She worked eighty-hour weeks not because she loved her job, but because achievement was the only thing that quieted the voice telling her she was worthless.

Isabella also overcompensated by being critical of others. If she could focus on others' flaws, maybe no one would notice hers. She had impossibly high standards for everyone, which kept people at a distance and protected her from intimacy.

Overcompensation + Dependence Schema

Yolanda grew up with overprotective parents who never let her do anything herself. She felt incompetent and helpless. As an adult, she overcompensated by being fiercely independent—to an unhealthy degree.

She refused help even when she needed it. She had to do everything herself to prove she was capable. She wouldn't ask for directions, wouldn't delegate at work, wouldn't let partners help with anything. She'd struggle with heavy furniture alone rather than admit she needed assistance.

Yolanda's overcompensation looked like strength, but it was exhausting and isolating. She couldn't accept help because it would trigger feelings of incompetence. She couldn't be vulnerable because it felt like admitting the schema was true.

Overcompensation + Failure Schema

Omar believed he was inadequate and would fail. His overcompensation looked like workaholism and obsessive achievement. He worked constantly, pushed himself relentlessly, couldn't rest or celebrate successes. He was always chasing the next accomplishment to prove he wasn't a failure.

But no achievement was ever enough. Omar would reach a goal, feel brief satisfaction, and then immediately focus on the next challenge. The relief from proving he wasn't a failure lasted only moments before the anxiety returned.

Omar also overcompensated by taking on too much. He said yes to every project, every opportunity, every request. He had to prove he was competent by being everywhere, doing everything. But he was burning out, and his overextension meant he sometimes did drop balls, which reinforced his failure schema.

Overcompensation + Subjugation Schema

Natasha grew up suppressing her needs to avoid punishment. As an adult, she overcompensated by being aggressive and demanding. She wouldn't take no for an answer. She bulldozed over others' boundaries. She insisted on getting her way.

But Natasha's assertiveness wasn't healthy confidence—it was a reaction against the terror of being controlled. She was so afraid of subjugation that she went too far in the other direction, becoming controlling herself.

In relationships, Natasha dominated. She made all the decisions, dismissed her partner's input, and reacted with rage if anyone tried to control her. This pushed people away and prevented genuine partnership.

Why Overcompensation Keeps You Stuck:

Overcompensation seems like it should work. You're actively fighting the schema, right? But here's the problem: overcompensation is still driven by the schema. You're reacting to it, letting it control you, just in a different way.

Isabella's perfectionism was still about defectiveness—she was just trying to hide it instead of accepting it. Tyler's leaving first was still about abandonment—he was just trying to control it instead of experiencing it. Natasha's aggressiveness was still about subjugation—she was just rebelling instead of surrendering.

Overcompensation is exhausting. It requires constant vigilance and effort. You can never relax because you're always fighting against the schema. And the more you fight, the more power you give the schema.

Also, overcompensation often creates new problems. Isabella's perfectionism led to anxiety and burnout. Tyler's leaving first meant he never had lasting relationships. Natasha's aggression alienated people. The overcompensation "solution" became its own problem.

The Same Schema, Three Different Coping Styles

Let's look at one schema—abandonment—with all three coping styles to see how different they are:

Surrender (Alex): "People will leave me, and there's nothing I can do about it. I'll just accept that relationships don't last." Alex doesn't try to maintain relationships and passively accepts their end.

Avoidance (Spencer): "If I never get attached, I can't be abandoned. I'll stay emotionally disconnected and avoid close relationships." Spencer protects himself by never letting anyone in.

Overcompensation (Tyler): "I'll leave before they can leave me. I'll stay in control so I'm never vulnerable to abandonment." Tyler ends relationships at the first sign of trouble.

All three are dealing with the same abandonment schema. All three developed a strategy to cope with the painful fear of being left. But all three strategies prevent healing and keep the schema active.

Mixing Coping Styles

Most people don't use just one coping style. You might surrender to one schema, avoid another, and overcompensate for a third. You might even use different coping styles with the same schema in different situations.

Claire had both abandonment and defectiveness schemas. She surrendered to the defectiveness (accepting that she was flawed and choosing partners who confirmed it), but she overcompensated for the abandonment (becoming controlling and jealous to prevent being left). She'd stay in relationships with people who treated her poorly (surrender to defectiveness) while frantically trying to control them to prevent them from leaving (overcompensation for abandonment).

You might also shift coping styles over time. Jacob used to surrender to his failure schema, accepting that he was incompetent. But after hitting rock bottom, he switched to overcompensation, becoming a workaholic overachiever. He was still driven by the same schema—just coping differently.

Coping Styles in Relationships: The Dance

Coping styles create patterns in relationships. Often, people's coping styles complement each other in unhealthy ways.

The Pursuer-Distancer Dance:

Lauren had an abandonment schema and coped by surrendering— she became clingy, needy, constantly seeking reassurance (also called "Compliant Surrenderer" mode). Her boyfriend Marco had an enmeshment schema and coped by overcompensating—he needed space, independence, emotional distance.

The more Lauren pursued, the more Marco distanced. The more Marco distanced, the more abandoned Lauren felt, so she pursued harder. Neither could stop the dance because each person's behavior triggered the other's schema.

The Caretaker-Receiver Dance:

Whitney had a self-sacrifice schema and coped by surrendering to it—she took care of everyone. Her husband Derek had a dependence schema and coped by surrendering—he let people take care of him. Whitney did everything for Derek, which prevented him from developing competence, which made him more dependent, which gave Whitney more to do.

Both stayed stuck. Whitney felt needed (which temporarily soothed her self-sacrifice schema) but also resentful. Derek felt taken care of (which prevented his dependence schema from being triggered) but also incompetent.

The Critic-Criticized Dance:

Aaron had an unrelenting standards schema and coped by overcompensating—he was perfectionistic and critical. His wife Simone had a defectiveness schema and coped by surrendering—she accepted that she wasn't good enough. Aaron's criticism confirmed Simone's defectiveness, and Simone's acceptance of criticism confirmed Aaron's belief that his standards were justified.

The Cost of Coping

All three coping styles come with costs:

Surrender costs you agency and hope. You accept the schema as truth and stop trying to change things. You miss opportunities because you've decided they won't work out anyway.

Avoidance costs you life experiences and emotional depth. You stay safe, but you also stay stuck. You miss connection, growth, and healing because you're too busy running away.

Overcompensation costs you energy and authenticity. You're constantly fighting, defending, proving. You can never relax into who you really are because you're busy being the opposite of your schema.

All three coping styles keep you focused on the schema. Whether you're surrendering to it, avoiding it, or fighting it, the schema is still running your life.

Exercise: Identifying Your Coping Styles

For each schema you identified in Chapter 3, ask yourself:

Do I surrender to this schema?

- Do I accept this schema as true?
- Do I behave in ways that confirm it?
- Do I choose situations that reinforce it?
- Do I give up trying to change it?

Do I avoid this schema?

- Do I stay away from situations that might trigger it?
- Do I shut down emotionally when it gets activated?
- Do I use substances, activities, or distractions to avoid feeling it?
- Do I isolate myself to prevent the schema from being triggered?

Do I overcompensate for this schema?

- Do I act the opposite of what the schema predicts?
- Am I driven to prove the schema wrong?
- Is my behavior extreme or rigid in the opposite direction?
- Am I fighting constantly against the schema?

Write down specific examples of each coping style. For instance:

"I have an abandonment schema. I cope by:

- Surrendering: Accepting that relationships won't last, not investing emotionally
- Avoiding: Staying busy so I don't notice loneliness, emotionally shutting down when someone gets close
- Overcompensating: Leaving relationships first, being controlling to prevent being left"

Understanding your coping styles is key to changing them. You can't heal a schema if you're busy avoiding, surrendering to, or fighting it. You need to face it directly, which we'll learn how to do in the healing chapters.

From Coping to Healing

Here's the hopeful part: coping styles are habits, and habits can be changed. You developed these strategies when you were young and had limited options. They made sense then. They kept you safe.

But now you're an adult with more resources, more understanding, and more choices. You don't need those old coping strategies anymore. You can learn new ways to respond to schemas—ways that actually lead to healing instead of reinforcement.

The first step is recognizing when you're using a coping style. When you notice yourself surrendering, avoiding, or overcompensating, you can pause and ask: "Is this helping me heal, or is this keeping me stuck?"

That pause—that moment of awareness—is where change begins.

In the next chapters, we'll look at schema modes (the different emotional states you shift between) and then specific techniques for healing. But understanding your coping styles is fundamental. These patterns are so automatic that you don't even notice them. Now that you see them, you can start to change them.

You've spent years protecting yourself. It makes sense. You did what you had to do.

Now it's time to learn that you don't need as much protection as you thought. You're stronger than the child who developed these schemas. You can handle the feelings you've been avoiding, surrendering to, or fighting against.

You can heal.

Chapter 5: Schema Modes

You've learned about schemas—those deep patterns from childhood. You've seen how you cope with them through surrender, avoidance, or overcompensation. Now let's talk about something you experience every single day, probably without realizing it: schema modes.

Modes are the different emotional states you shift between. Think of them as different versions of yourself that take over at different times. One minute you're functioning well, making decisions, handling life. The next minute you feel like a scared child. An hour later you're furiously angry. Then you shut down completely and feel nothing.

These aren't personality disorders or signs that something's wrong with you. These are normal responses to schema activation. Everyone has modes. The question is: which modes do you get stuck in, and how much control does your Healthy Adult have?

Why Modes Matter

Dr. Young developed the concept of modes because schemas alone couldn't explain what he was seeing in therapy. Patients—especially those with borderline personality disorder—would shift rapidly between emotional states. One session they'd be crying and vulnerable. The next session they'd be angry and aggressive. Then they'd shut down completely.

These weren't different people. These were different modes—combinations of schemas, emotions, and coping styles that would activate depending on the situation.

Understanding modes helps in three ways:

First, it normalizes your experience. Instead of thinking "I'm crazy" or "I'm unstable," you can think, "Oh, my Angry Child mode got triggered" or "I'm in Detached Protector mode right now." This creates distance and perspective.

Second, it helps you track patterns. Once you can identify modes, you'll notice what triggers them and how long they last. You'll see the sequence: "When my boss criticizes me, I go into Vulnerable Child mode, then I flip into Punitive Parent mode where I beat myself up."

Third, it gives you something concrete to work with. You can't easily "fix" an abandonment schema. But you can learn to recognize when your Vulnerable Child mode is active and respond to it with your Healthy Adult mode.

The Four Categories of Modes

Schema therapy identifies four main categories of modes: Child modes, Dysfunctional Coping modes, Dysfunctional Parent modes, and the Healthy Adult mode.

Let's explore each one.

Child Modes: The Core of Your Emotions

Child modes are where your primary emotions live. When you're in a child mode, you're experiencing emotions with the intensity and perspective of the child you once were. These aren't childish reactions—they're genuine emotional responses that feel overwhelming because they're connected to old wounds.

There are four main child modes:

Vulnerable Child Mode

This is the mode where you feel small, scared, hurt, alone, or helpless. It's the emotional state of a child whose needs aren't being met.

What it feels like:

- Abandoned, lonely, isolated
- Scared, anxious, panicky
- Sad, hurt, rejected
- Helpless, powerless, small
- Needy, desperate for comfort
- Unlovable, worthless

When it gets triggered:

Monica's Vulnerable Child mode activated whenever she sensed distance from her boyfriend. If he seemed distracted during dinner, if he didn't text back quickly, if he made plans without her—suddenly Monica felt like that seven-year-old whose mother would disappear for days during manic episodes. The adult understanding that her boyfriend was just busy at work couldn't reach her. In Vulnerable Child mode, she felt abandoned and terrified.

Frank's Vulnerable Child came out when he made mistakes at work. A small error would trigger overwhelming shame and fear. He'd feel like the child whose father would explode in rage over spilled milk. Even though his current boss was patient and understanding, Frank couldn't access that reality when his Vulnerable Child was activated.

What it looks like to others:

When someone is in Vulnerable Child mode, they might cry easily, seek reassurance repeatedly, or seem fragile and needy. They might look younger—their voice changes, their posture becomes smaller, their facial expressions look childlike. People often say, "You look like a little kid right now" or "It's like I'm talking to a different person."

The important thing to understand:

Your Vulnerable Child isn't weakness. It's the part of you that holds pain from the past. This mode needs compassion, not criticism. When your Vulnerable Child is activated, you need comfort and reassurance—from yourself or others—not lectures about being logical or tough.

Angry Child Mode

This mode emerges when the Vulnerable Child's needs have been ignored, dismissed, or violated. It's rage that comes from repeated hurt and frustration.

What it feels like:

- Intense anger or rage
- Frustration, impatience
- A sense of injustice or unfairness
- Explosive, out-of-control feelings
- "I've had enough" energy

When it gets triggered:

Corey's Angry Child exploded when he felt criticized. His girlfriend made a mild comment about him forgetting to call, and suddenly Corey was yelling. His anger was way bigger than the situation warranted. That's because it wasn't really about the phone call—it was about all the times his mother criticized him as a child, all the times he felt nothing he did was good enough.

Diana's Angry Child came out when people didn't listen to her. She'd be in a meeting, make a suggestion that got ignored, and feel volcanic rage building. She'd fantasize about yelling at everyone, sometimes she'd storm out. Her anger was connected to growing up with parents who dismissed everything she said, who acted like her opinions didn't matter.

What it looks like to others:

In Angry Child mode, people might yell, slam doors, throw things, or say hurtful things they later regret. The anger feels uncontrolled and disproportionate to the trigger. Afterward, they might feel guilty or confused about why they reacted so strongly.

The important thing to understand:

Angry Child isn't bad or wrong. It's actually protective—it's trying to defend the Vulnerable Child. The problem is that adult situations don't usually require this level of rage, and expressing anger this way often creates more problems. Your Angry Child needs validation for the hurt underneath the anger, and then help expressing needs in a healthier way.

Impulsive/Undisciplined Child Mode

This mode wants what it wants right now. It acts without thinking about consequences. It's driven by immediate gratification and has little frustration tolerance.

What it feels like:

- "I want it now"
- "I shouldn't have to wait"
- "This is boring, I'm done"
- Restless, impatient energy
- Entitled to immediate pleasure

When it gets triggered:

Keith's Impulsive Child took over whenever he felt stressed or bored. He'd quit jobs without another lined up. He'd spend money he didn't have. He'd start projects enthusiastically and abandon them when they got difficult. He'd eat entire pizzas, drink too much, or stay up gaming until 4am even though he had work the next day.

Priya's Impulsive Child came out in relationships. When she was frustrated with her partner, instead of talking about it, she'd impulsively break up. When she met someone new and exciting, she'd jump into bed immediately without thinking. When things got boring or hard, she'd look for the next exciting thing.

What it looks like to others:

People in Impulsive Child mode seem irresponsible, reckless, or unable to delay gratification. They start things and don't finish them.

They make impulsive decisions that create problems later. They can't tolerate boredom or frustration.

The important thing to understand:

Impulsive Child often develops when there weren't consistent limits and structure in childhood, or when life was so chaotic that long-term planning felt pointless. This mode needs help learning that good things can come from patience and that you can tolerate uncomfortable feelings without acting on them immediately.

Happy Child Mode

This is the only healthy child mode. It's when you feel loved, safe, content, playful, and free.

What it feels like:

- Joyful, excited, playful
- Safe, protected, loved
- Spontaneous, creative
- Connected to others
- Optimistic about life
- Free to be yourself

When it shows up:

Tasha's Happy Child came out when she was painting. She'd lose track of time, getting absorbed in colors and shapes. She felt playful and free, not worried about whether it was "good enough." This was the part of her that never got crushed by her critical parents.

Luis's Happy Child emerged when he was playing with his kids. He'd wrestle with them, make up silly voices, laugh genuinely. For those moments, he wasn't the anxious, stressed adult worried about bills and responsibilities. He was just present and joyful.

What it looks like to others:

In Happy Child mode, people are lighter, more spontaneous, more genuine. They laugh easily, play without self-consciousness, and enjoy the moment without worrying about the future. They look younger in a positive way—relaxed and open.

The important thing to understand:

Many people with strong schemas rarely access their Happy Child. Life feels too serious, too dangerous, too much work. One goal of schema therapy is to help you reconnect with this mode—to find moments of genuine joy, play, and spontaneity. Your Happy Child is still in there, even if it's been buried for years.

Dysfunctional Coping Modes: Your Survival Strategies

These modes are the ways you've learned to cope with painful child modes. They're the armor you put on to avoid feeling vulnerable. Remember the three coping styles from Chapter 4? They show up as specific modes.

Compliant Surrenderer Mode

This is the surrender coping style in action. In this mode, you give in, submit, and accept poor treatment. You become passive and compliant.

What it looks like:

Tracy's Compliant Surrenderer took over in her relationship with her domineering husband. She'd agree to whatever he wanted, even when she disagreed. She'd apologize for things that weren't her fault. She'd accept blame and criticism without defending herself. She'd do all the emotional and household labor without complaint.

In this mode, Tracy's voice even changed—becoming softer, more uncertain. She'd say things like "I don't know" or "Whatever you think" or "I'm sorry" constantly. She looked defeated, shoulders slumped, avoiding eye contact.

Why this mode developed:

Tracy grew up with an angry father. Complying kept her safe. Arguing or asserting herself led to punishment. Her Compliant Surrenderer mode protected her Vulnerable Child from her father's rage. The problem was, she was still using this protection as an adult, even though her husband wasn't actually dangerous—just difficult.

The cost:

People stuck in Compliant Surrenderer mode lose themselves. They don't express needs, don't set boundaries, don't pursue their own goals. They build up massive resentment that has nowhere to go. Eventually, they might explode (Angry Child) or shut down completely (next mode).

Detached Protector Mode

This is the avoidance coping style in action. In this mode, you disconnect emotionally. You feel numb, empty, or robotic. You're going through the motions but not really present.

What it looks like:

When things got overwhelming, Raymond's Detached Protector would kick in. He'd feel nothing. His voice would become flat and emotionless. He'd go through his day on autopilot—work, dinner, TV, sleep—but he wasn't really there. People would talk to him and he'd barely register their words.

In this mode, Raymond avoided anything that might trigger feelings. He'd cancel plans with friends. He'd zone out in conversations. He'd spend hours scrolling on his phone or watching shows he didn't even enjoy. He was hiding from life.

Why this mode developed:

Raymond experienced trauma as a child. The feelings were too overwhelming to process, so he learned to shut them down. Detached Protector was his mind's way of protecting him from unbearable pain. If you don't feel, you can't hurt.

The cost:

The Detached Protector might protect you from pain, but it also blocks joy, connection, and meaning. People in this mode feel dead inside. They go through life without experiencing it. They're safe but lonely, protected but empty.

Overcompensator Mode

This is the overcompensation coping style in action. In this mode, you fight against your schemas by doing the opposite. You might become controlling, aggressive, competitive, perfectionistic, or superior.

What it looks like:

Gordon had deep feelings of defectiveness underneath. His Overcompensator mode protected him by making him appear perfect. He dressed impeccably, achieved at the highest levels, corrected others' mistakes, and presented an image of complete competence. If someone suggested he'd made an error, he'd become defensive and find ways to blame them or circumstances.

Simone's Overcompensator protected her abandonment fears by making her the one in control. She'd dominate relationships, make all decisions, and keep emotional distance. She appeared strong and independent, but underneath she was terrified of needing someone.

Why this mode developed:

Overcompensator modes develop when surrender and avoidance don't feel safe enough. Instead of accepting the schema or avoiding it, you rebel against it. You prove it wrong through extreme behavior in the opposite direction.

The cost:

Overcompensator modes are exhausting. You can never relax because you're always fighting, proving, maintaining the image. Plus, these modes often hurt relationships. Gordon's perfectionism made people feel criticized and inadequate. Simone's control pushed partners away. The overcompensation prevents genuine connection.

Other Coping Modes

There are several other coping modes worth mentioning:

Angry Protector: Uses anger to keep people at a distance and avoid vulnerable feelings. Different from Angry Child (which is pure hurt), this is strategic anger used as protection. Wallace would pick fights whenever someone got too close emotionally. His anger kept people away before they could hurt him.

Self-Soother: Uses addictive behaviors to numb feelings—food, alcohol, drugs, shopping, sex, gambling, gaming. Iris's Self-Soother mode had her eating entire pints of ice cream while watching TV until she felt nothing. The behavior soothed painful emotions temporarily but created new problems.

Paranoid Overcontroller: Developed from mistrust schema, this mode is hypervigilant and suspicious, trying to control everything to stay safe. Derek planned every detail obsessively, trusted no one fully, and constantly looked for hidden motives. His overcontrol was exhausting but felt necessary.

Dysfunctional Parent Modes: The Critical Voices

These modes are internalized voices from your actual parents or other authority figures. They're the messages you heard so often as a child that they became your own thoughts.

Parent modes are tricky because they feel like truth, like your own opinions. But they're actually introjects—absorbed beliefs from others that aren't genuinely yours.

Punitive Parent Mode

This is the harsh, critical, punishing voice that attacks you for mistakes, feelings, or needs.

What it sounds like:

"You're so stupid. How could you be such an idiot?" "You deserve to suffer for what you did." "You're disgusting. You should be ashamed." "You're weak. Stop crying and toughen up." "You'll never amount to anything."

What it looks like:

When Veronica made mistakes, her Punitive Parent would attack viciously. She'd call herself names, sometimes out loud. She'd refuse to eat or sleep as punishment. She'd ruminate on her failures for days, mentally beating herself up. She felt she deserved the punishment—that's what made it so insidious.

After Garrett failed an exam, his Punitive Parent told him he was worthless and should just drop out. He felt crushing shame and self-hatred. He couldn't access self-compassion or perspective. The Punitive Parent was so loud that it drowned out everything else.

Where it comes from:

Punitive Parent modes usually come from harsh, critical, or abusive parents. But they can also come from other sources—strict religious environments, military training, bullying, or perfectionistic cultures. The critical voice gets internalized, and now you do to yourself what others once did to you.

The cost:

The Punitive Parent is devastating. It makes you feel worthless, ashamed, and deserving of punishment. It prevents healing because it attacks the vulnerable parts of you that need compassion. It's like having an abuser living in your head, constantly tearing you down.

Demanding Parent Mode

This voice pushes you to achieve more, be better, work harder. It's never satisfied with your efforts.

What it sounds like:

"That's not good enough. You can do better." "You're lazy. You should be working harder." "Other people are more successful than you. What's wrong with you?" "You don't have time to rest. There's too much to do." "If you just tried harder, you'd be successful."

What it looks like:

Carmen's Demanding Parent never let her rest. She'd finish a big project and immediately focus on the next one, never celebrating her achievement. She worked twelve-hour days, exercised every morning, kept her house spotless, and still felt behind. The voice kept pushing: "More. Better. Faster."

Quinn's Demanding Parent compared him constantly to others. Friends getting promotions, siblings buying houses, colleagues publishing papers—everyone else's success made him feel inadequate. He couldn't enjoy his own life because he was too busy measuring himself against others and coming up short.

Where it comes from:

Demanding Parent modes often come from parents who had impossibly high standards, gave conditional love based on achievement, or constantly pushed for more. The message was: you're only worthwhile if you're achieving.

The cost:

The Demanding Parent creates chronic dissatisfaction, anxiety, and exhaustion. Nothing is ever good enough. You can't relax or enjoy life because you're always chasing the next goal. This mode is a major source of burnout and depression.

Healthy Adult Mode: Your Goal

This is the mode you're working toward. It's the integrated, balanced, functional part of you that can handle life's challenges while also nurturing your emotional needs.

What Healthy Adult looks like:

The Healthy Adult mode:

- **Makes decisions** based on values and long-term goals, not fear or impulse
- **Handles responsibilities** without being driven or perfectionistic
- **Sets boundaries** without being aggressive or submissive
- **Expresses needs** clearly and directly
- **Nurtures the Vulnerable Child** with compassion
- **Validates the Angry Child** while channeling anger appropriately
- **Limits the Impulsive Child** with gentle firmness
- **Stands up to the Punitive Parent** and refuses the attacks
- **Negotiates with the Demanding Parent** for reasonable standards
- **Replaces Dysfunctional Coping modes** with healthy coping
- **Connects with the Happy Child** through play and spontaneity

What it sounds like:

"This is hard, but I can handle it." "I'm allowed to make mistakes. That's how I learn." "I feel scared right now, but I'm safe. I can comfort myself." "I'm angry about this, and that's okay. Let me figure out how to address it constructively." "I need to take care of myself right now, and that's not selfish." "This person's criticism is about them, not about my worth."

An example of Healthy Adult in action:

Brianna got critical feedback from her boss. In the past, this would trigger a chain reaction:

- First, Vulnerable Child: "I'm not good enough. I'm going to get fired."
- Then, Punitive Parent: "You're such a failure. You're incompetent."
- Then, either Compliant Surrenderer: giving up and accepting the criticism as complete truth, or Overcompensator: getting defensive and blaming others.

But Brianna had been working on developing her Healthy Adult mode. This time, she noticed the familiar chain starting and consciously interrupted it:

Healthy Adult to Vulnerable Child: "I know this feels scary, like when Dad used to criticize you. But this is different. Your boss is giving you feedback on one project, not saying you're worthless. You're not in danger."

Healthy Adult to Punitive Parent: "Stop. I'm not listening to you call me names. That's not helpful, and it's not true."

Healthy Adult to the situation: "Okay, let me look at this feedback objectively. Some points are valid and I can learn from them. Some points I disagree with, and I can discuss that with my boss. This is normal work feedback, not a catastrophe."

She felt the emotions—disappointment, some shame, worry—but didn't get consumed by them. She made a plan to address the feedback and scheduled time with her boss to discuss it. Then she went home and did something nice for herself instead of ruminating all evening.

That's Healthy Adult in action.

Tracking Your Modes

The best way to understand your modes is to start noticing them in real time. Over the next week, keep a mode journal.

When you notice a shift in your emotional state, write down:

What happened? (the trigger) "My partner said he needed space tonight to work on a project."

What mode did I go into? "Vulnerable Child—I felt abandoned and panicky."

How did I know? "My chest got tight, I felt like crying, I wanted to text him repeatedly to make sure he wasn't mad at me. I felt like a little kid."

What other modes showed up? "Then Punitive Parent came in: 'You're too needy. No wonder he wants space.' Then Compliant Surrenderer: 'I should just accept that I'm alone and stop bothering him.'"

How long did it last? "About two hours."

What helped me shift? "I called my friend who reminded me this is normal and doesn't mean he's leaving. I used some Healthy Adult self-talk: 'He's working on a project, not abandoning you. You can be alone for one evening.'"

The more you track, the more patterns you'll see. You might notice:

- Certain people or situations trigger specific modes
- You have a common sequence (Vulnerable Child → Punitive Parent → Detached Protector)
- Some modes are harder to shift out of than others
- Your Healthy Adult is stronger at certain times of day or in certain situations

Mode Dialogues: Talking Between Parts

One powerful technique is having conversations between your modes. This might sound strange, but it helps create separation and understanding.

Example: Xavier's mode dialogue

Xavier's girlfriend canceled plans because she wasn't feeling well. His Vulnerable Child went into panic mode.

Vulnerable Child: "She doesn't want to see me. She's going to leave me. I'm going to be alone forever."

Punitive Parent: "You're being pathetic. Stop being so needy and clingy. This is why people leave you."

Healthy Adult (to Vulnerable Child): "I hear that you're scared. I know this reminds you of when Mom used to cancel plans and then disappear for days. But your girlfriend isn't Mom. She's sick. She still cares about you."

Vulnerable Child: "But what if she's lying? What if this is the beginning of her pulling away?"

Healthy Adult: "That's possible, but unlikely. She's been consistent for six months. One canceled plan doesn't mean abandonment. Let's look at the evidence."

Healthy Adult (to Punitive Parent): "Stop attacking him. Feeling scared doesn't make someone pathetic. His fears make sense given his history. We're going to handle this with compassion, not criticism."

Punitive Parent: "But he needs to toughen up—"

Healthy Adult: "No. We're done with that approach. It doesn't help. We're going to comfort the scared part and then respond rationally to the situation."

Healthy Adult (decision): "We're going to text her something supportive: 'Sorry you're not feeling well. Rest up, and let me know if you need anything.' Then we're going to do something nice for ourselves tonight instead of ruminating. We're going to trust that this relationship is okay."

This might seem like you're talking to yourself, and you are. But it's a structured way of organizing the different parts of your internal experience and letting your Healthy Adult take charge.

The Goal: Healthy Adult in Charge

You'll never eliminate your other modes. The Vulnerable Child will always exist—those old wounds are part of your story. The Angry Child will still show up when you're hurt. The Punitive Parent's voice might pop up when you make mistakes.

That's okay. That's normal.

The goal isn't to make those modes disappear. The goal is to develop a strong Healthy Adult mode that can:

- Notice when other modes are active
- Understand what triggered them
- Respond with compassion and wisdom
- Keep those modes from running your life

Think of it like this: Imagine all your modes are people in a car. For most of your life, the Vulnerable Child or Punitive Parent or Detached Protector has been driving while your Healthy Adult sat in the back seat, barely aware they existed.

Schema therapy is about getting your Healthy Adult into the driver's seat. The other modes are still in the car—they're not going anywhere—but now a competent adult is steering, with a clear view of the road and a good sense of where you're going.

Sometimes a child mode will still grab the wheel and swerve the car. That happens. But as your Healthy Adult gets stronger, you'll notice faster, take back control sooner, and handle it more skillfully.

Exercise: Meet Your Modes

Grab your notebook and answer these questions:

Which child modes do you experience most often?

- Do you spend time in Vulnerable Child? What triggers it?
- Does your Angry Child come out? When and how?
- Do you have an Impulsive Child that takes over? What happens?
- Can you access your Happy Child? When was the last time?

Which coping modes do you use?

- Do you go into Compliant Surrenderer? With whom?
- Does Detached Protector shut you down? What triggers it?
- Do you use an Overcompensator mode? What does it look like?

What do your parent modes sound like?

- Do you have a Punitive Parent? Write down its exact words.
- Do you have a Demanding Parent? What does it demand?

How strong is your Healthy Adult?

- In what situations does your Healthy Adult show up?
- What helps you access this mode?
- What makes it harder to stay in Healthy Adult?

Understanding your modes is like getting a map of your internal world. Now when emotions hit, you won't just feel overwhelmed—you'll understand what's happening and have tools to work with it.

In the next chapter, we'll get into the specific techniques for healing schemas and strengthening your Healthy Adult. You're ready.

Chapter 6: Schema Therapy Techniques

Now comes the part you've been waiting for: how do you actually heal these schemas? How do you change patterns that have been running your life for decades?

The answer is both simple and difficult. Simple because the techniques aren't complicated. Difficult because they require you to face painful emotions, challenge deep beliefs, and practice new behaviors repeatedly until they become natural.

Schema therapy uses three main types of techniques: cognitive (working with thoughts), experiential (working with emotions), and behavioral (working with actions). You need all three. Thinking about your schemas isn't enough. Feeling your emotions isn't enough. Changing behavior isn't enough. Real healing happens when you work with thoughts, feelings, and actions together.

Let's explore each type.

Cognitive Techniques: Working With Your Thoughts

Cognitive techniques help you identify schema-driven thoughts and test whether they're actually true. Your schemas act like filters, showing you distorted versions of reality. Cognitive work helps you see more clearly.

Technique 1: Schema Awareness and Labeling

The first step is recognizing when a schema is active. Once you can label it, you create distance from it.

How it works:

Instead of thinking "I'm unlovable" (which feels like truth), you learn to think "My defectiveness schema is activated right now" (which feels like an observation).

This shift is powerful. "I'm unlovable" is you. "My schema is active" is something happening to you—something you can observe and work with.

Practice:

When you notice intense emotions or unhelpful thoughts, ask yourself: "Which schema might be driving this?"

Marcus got anxious when his girlfriend didn't text back for a few hours. His first thought was: "She's pulling away. This is the beginning of the end."

Old Marcus would have spiraled into that thought, maybe sent multiple texts, maybe picked a fight out of anxiety.

New Marcus, practicing schema awareness, caught the thought and labeled it: "Oh, this is my abandonment schema. I'm interpreting normal behavior as rejection because of my history. The schema is running, but that doesn't mean it's right."

Just labeling the schema helped Marcus calm down enough to think more clearly.

Technique 2: Evidence For and Against

Schemas make you biased. You notice evidence that confirms them and ignore evidence that contradicts them. This technique forces you to look at both sides.

How it works:

Take a schema-driven belief and examine it objectively. What's the evidence it's true? What's the evidence it's false?

Practice:

Josephine believed "I always fail at important things" (failure schema). Her therapist had her write down evidence:

Evidence FOR "I always fail":

- I dropped out of college after one semester
- I've been fired from two jobs
- My last relationship ended badly
- I started a business that went under

Evidence AGAINST "I always fail":

- I went back and finished my degree, graduated with honors
- I've held my current job successfully for three years and got promoted
- I have two close friendships that have lasted over a decade
- I learned guitar and can play well enough to perform at open mics
- I raised two children who are doing well
- I bought a house and managed the entire process

Looking at the list, Josephine could see that her failure schema was selective. Yes, she'd had failures—everyone does. But she'd also had significant successes that her schema had been filtering out.

The realization didn't instantly heal her schema, but it planted doubt in the schema's absolute truth. That doubt created space for change.

Technique 3: The Healthy Adult Response

This technique involves writing out what your Healthy Adult would say in response to schema-driven thoughts.

How it works:

When your Punitive Parent attacks or your schemas predict catastrophe, your Healthy Adult writes a response that's both compassionate and realistic.

Practice:

Winston's Punitive Parent would attack him viciously when he made mistakes: "You're incompetent. You should be ashamed. Everyone can see what a fraud you are."

His therapist had him write out Healthy Adult responses:

Punitive Parent: "You messed up that presentation. You're a complete failure."

Healthy Adult: "I made some mistakes in the presentation, yes. I was nervous and lost my train of thought. That's human. It doesn't mean I'm a failure. It means I had an off day. I've given dozens of good presentations. This one wasn't my best, but I can learn from it and do better next time. Making mistakes doesn't make me incompetent—it makes me human."

Winston kept these responses on his phone. When the Punitive Parent attacked, he'd read his Healthy Adult response out loud. Over time, the Healthy Adult voice got stronger and more automatic.

Technique 4: Historical Role-Play

This technique helps you see how your schemas developed—and why they made sense at the time but don't apply anymore.

How it works:

You have a conversation between your child self and your current adult self, helping the child understand what was really happening.

Practice:

Ingrid had a defectiveness schema from growing up with a highly critical mother. Her therapist had her do this exercise:

Adult Ingrid to Child Ingrid: "Why do you think Mom criticized you so much?"

Child Ingrid: "Because I wasn't good enough. If I tried harder, she'd love me more."

Adult Ingrid: "Actually, Mom had depression and anxiety. She was unhappy with her own life, and she took it out on you. Her criticism was about her problems, not about you being defective."

Child Ingrid: "But she said I was lazy and selfish and difficult."

Adult Ingrid: "She said those things, yes. But they weren't true. You were a normal kid. All kids are sometimes lazy and selfish— that's development, not defectiveness. Mom needed someone to be perfect so she could feel okay about herself. That wasn't fair to put on a child. You deserved unconditional love, and you didn't get it. That was her failure, not yours."

This conversation helped Ingrid separate her mother's issues from her own worth. She started seeing her schema as a misunderstanding rather than truth.

Experiential Techniques: Working With Your Emotions

Cognitive techniques work with thoughts, but schemas aren't just thoughts—they're emotional memories. You might intellectually understand your schema is wrong, but you still feel it's true. That's where experiential techniques come in.

These techniques activate emotions so you can process and heal them. They might feel awkward or intense, but they're powerful.

Technique 5: Imagery Rescripting

This is one of the most powerful schema therapy techniques. You revisit painful childhood memories in imagination and change them—not to pretend they didn't happen, but to give your child self what was needed at the time.

How it works:

You close your eyes and imagine a specific childhood memory where a schema was formed or reinforced. Then you imagine your adult self entering the scene and intervening—protecting, comforting, or advocating for your child self.

Practice:

Lawrence had a memory of being eight years old, getting called to the principal's office for something he didn't do. His father came to the school, listened to the principal, and without asking Lawrence's side of the story, yelled at him and punished him. Lawrence felt helpless, undefended, and assumed he must have deserved it.

In therapy, Lawrence revisited this memory in imagery:

First, he re-experienced it as it happened, feeling the child's fear and hurt.

Then, his therapist guided him to imagine adult Lawrence entering the scene.

Adult Lawrence walked into the principal's office, put his hand on young Lawrence's shoulder, and said, "Hold on. Let's hear what actually happened."

He listened to young Lawrence's explanation. Then he turned to the father: "You made a mistake. You didn't ask for his side of the story. You just assumed he was guilty. That wasn't fair. He's your son, and he needed you to believe him and defend him."

To the principal: "You need to investigate properly before accusing students."

To young Lawrence: "I believe you. I know you didn't do this. You don't deserve to be punished. I'm going to take you out of here. You're safe with me."

In the imagery, adult Lawrence took young Lawrence out for ice cream and told him: "Your father was wrong. He should have listened to you. That was his failure, not yours. You're a good kid."

After this exercise, Lawrence cried for twenty minutes—releasing decades of hurt. But something shifted. The memory still existed, but it felt different. It no longer had the same power to make him feel helpless and worthless.

Note: This technique should ideally be done with a therapist, especially for traumatic memories. But you can practice with less intense memories on your own.

Technique 6: Empty Chair Dialogues

In this technique, you have conversations with people from your past (or parts of yourself) using empty chairs to represent them.

How it works:

You put an empty chair across from you. You imagine someone sitting in it—maybe your critical father, maybe your neglectful mother, maybe your Punitive Parent mode. You talk to them, saying things you never got to say. Then you switch chairs and respond from their perspective. This creates new understanding and allows you to express long-suppressed emotions.

Practice:

Estelle's mother was emotionally cold and dismissive. Estelle never felt loved or valued. In therapy, she did an empty chair exercise:

Estelle (to empty chair representing mother): "I needed you. I needed you to hug me and tell me I mattered. I needed you to ask about my day and care about my feelings. But you never did. You acted like I was a burden. I spent my whole childhood trying to earn your love, and I never could. Do you have any idea how much that hurt?"

Then Estelle switched chairs and responded as her mother: "I... I didn't know how to show love. My parents didn't show me love either. I felt overwhelmed and depressed. I did the best I could, but it wasn't enough. I'm sorry."

Switching back to her own chair: "Your best wasn't good enough for a child. I deserved better. And your depression doesn't erase my pain. I'm angry at you, and I have a right to be angry."

This dialogue helped Estelle access and express years of suppressed hurt and anger. It also helped her develop some compassion for her mother while still honoring her own pain.

Technique 7: Limited Reparenting

This is a unique aspect of schema therapy. The therapist-patient relationship becomes a place where unmet childhood needs can be partially met.

How it works:

The therapist provides what the patient needed but didn't get as a child: unconditional positive regard, consistent support, appropriate guidance, and empathic understanding. They validate emotions, set healthy boundaries, and model the Healthy Adult.

This isn't friendship—it's a professional relationship with clear boundaries. But within those boundaries, the therapist offers a corrective emotional experience: "This is what it feels like to have someone truly care about your wellbeing without wanting something from you."

Why it matters:

Many people with strong schemas never experienced secure attachment. They don't know what healthy relationships feel like. The therapy relationship becomes a laboratory where they can experience and practice healthy relating.

Zara had never experienced unconditional acceptance. Her therapist provided that—consistently showing up, not judging her, accepting her emotions, believing in her potential even when Zara didn't.

Over time, Zara internalized this experience. She started treating herself with the same acceptance and compassion her therapist showed her. The therapy relationship taught her what was possible in relationships.

Note: If you're not in therapy, you can still seek out corrective relationships—with partners, friends, mentors, or support groups where you experience healthier patterns.

Behavioral Techniques: Working With Your Actions

Cognitive and experiential work create internal shifts, but you also need to change your behavior. You have to practice new ways of acting, even when it feels uncomfortable.

Behavioral techniques help you break old patterns and build new ones.

Technique 8: Behavioral Pattern-Breaking

This involves identifying behaviors driven by schemas and deliberately doing something different.

How it works:

You identify a schema-driven behavior, understand its purpose, and then experiment with a new behavior that gets your needs met more effectively.

Practice:

Nora had a self-sacrifice schema. Her pattern was to say yes to every request, even when she was overwhelmed. This behavior came from believing her needs didn't matter and that her worth came from helping others.

Behavioral pattern-breaking meant saying no—even when it felt terrifying.

Nora's friend asked her to help with a move on a weekend when Nora was already exhausted from work. Her automatic response was to say yes. But she caught herself.

Old behavior (schema-driven): "Of course! I'll be there!" **New behavior (pattern-breaking):** "I can't this weekend. I'm sorry."

Her friend said, "No problem, I'll ask someone else."

And that was it. The world didn't end. Her friend didn't hate her. Nora survived saying no.

This small experiment challenged her schema. Each time she said no and survived, her self-sacrifice schema weakened a bit.

Technique 9: Graded Exposure

When you avoid situations due to schemas, you need gradual exposure to face your fears and learn they're not as dangerous as you think.

How it works:

You create a hierarchy of feared situations from least to most scary. Then you practice them in order, starting with the easiest.

Practice:

Felix had social isolation and defectiveness schemas. He avoided social situations because he assumed he'd be rejected. His therapist helped him create an exposure hierarchy:

Level 1 (least scary): Make small talk with a cashier **Level 2:** Comment in an online forum **Level 3:** Attend a meetup group but leave after 30 minutes **Level 4:** Stay at the meetup for the full time **Level 5:** Invite someone from the meetup for coffee **Level 6:** Host a small gathering at his apartment **Level 7:** Share something personal in conversation **Level 8:** Handle potential rejection or criticism

Felix started with Level 1. Once he could do that comfortably, he moved to Level 2, and so on. Each successful exposure showed him that social situations weren't as dangerous as his schemas predicted.

Technique 10: Flash Cards

You create cards with schema-challenging messages and read them daily to reinforce new beliefs.

How it works:

You write out Healthy Adult responses to your schemas, including evidence against the schema and rational perspectives. You read these multiple times per day until the new thoughts become more automatic.

Practice:

Helena's abandonment schema told her she'd end up alone. She created a flash card:

Front: "What my abandonment schema says" "You'll end up alone. No one will stay. Everyone leaves eventually."

Back: "What my Healthy Adult knows" "This is my abandonment schema, not reality. Yes, some relationships have ended, but that's normal. I have friends who've been in my life for years. My sister is consistent. My partner has been reliable for two years. People don't leave just because I fear they will. I'm working on my clingy behaviors that used to push people away. I'm learning to tolerate normal distance without panicking. I can handle being alone when needed, and I also have people who care about me."

Helena read this card every morning and whenever her schema got triggered. Over time, the Healthy Adult perspective became stronger and more accessible.

Technique 11: Empathic Confrontation

This is something a therapist does, but you can also do it for yourself. It means compassionately but firmly confronting schema-driven behaviors.

How it works:

You acknowledge the pain and fear behind a behavior while also pointing out how that behavior is self-destructive.

Practice:

When Malcolm's girlfriend got busy with work, he'd bombard her with texts and get angry when she didn't respond immediately. His therapist confronted this gently:

"I understand you're scared. Your abandonment schema is screaming that she's pulling away. That fear is real and makes sense given your history. AND—sending twenty texts and getting angry is pushing her away. The behavior you're using to prevent abandonment is actually creating the distance you fear. We need to find a different way for you to handle these feelings."

Malcolm learned to do this for himself: "I'm scared right now, and that's okay. But I'm not going to text her again. That won't help. I'm going to sit with the uncomfortable feeling and trust that she'll respond when she can."

Putting Techniques Together: A Complete Example

Let's see how all three types of techniques work together with one person's schema.

Vanessa's Story:

Vanessa had strong defectiveness and failure schemas from growing up with a hypercritical mother. As an adult, she was underemployed, stayed in a relationship with someone who treated her poorly, and struggled with depression.

Cognitive work:

- She learned to identify when her schemas were active: "That's my defectiveness schema telling me I don't deserve better."
- She kept an evidence log of her competencies and positive qualities
- She developed Healthy Adult responses to her Punitive Parent's attacks
- She did historical role-play to understand her mother's criticism was about her mother's issues, not Vanessa's worth

Experiential work:

- She did imagery rescripting of a memory where her mother called her stupid and worthless. Adult Vanessa entered the scene, defended young Vanessa, and told her she was smart and valuable
- She did empty chair work, expressing anger at her mother and processing years of hurt
- She worked with a therapist who provided consistent validation and acceptance, giving her a corrective emotional experience

Behavioral work:

- She practiced saying no to her boyfriend's unreasonable demands
- She eventually left the relationship despite fear of being alone
- She applied for jobs that matched her qualifications instead of settling for less
- She exposed herself gradually to situations where she might be evaluated

- She used flash cards daily to reinforce her worth

The process took two years. It wasn't linear—she had setbacks and struggles. But slowly, the schemas weakened. Vanessa got a better job, started dating someone who treated her well, and developed genuine self-respect.

She still sometimes heard the Punitive Parent voice or felt defective. But now her Healthy Adult could step in quickly: "That's the schema. It's not the truth. I know my worth now."

Which Techniques Should You Use?

You don't need to use every technique. Different ones work for different people and different schemas.

If you're very cognitive and analytical: Start with cognitive techniques. They'll feel most comfortable.

If you're disconnected from emotions: Focus on experiential techniques, even though they'll be uncomfortable. You need to feel to heal.

If you understand your patterns but can't change them: Focus on behavioral techniques. Knowledge without action won't create change.

If you're overwhelmed by emotions: Start with cognitive techniques to create some distance, then move to experiential work when you're ready.

If you're working on your own: Focus on cognitive techniques, flash cards, behavioral experiments, and basic imagery work. Save deeper experiential techniques for work with a therapist.

If you're in therapy: Use all three types with your therapist's guidance.

Important Reminders

Progress isn't linear. You'll have good days and bad days. You'll make progress and then slide backward. That's normal. Healing isn't a straight line.

Emotions will intensify before they improve. When you start doing experiential work, old feelings surface. This can feel worse before it feels better. That's actually a sign the work is happening.

You need repetition. Doing an exercise once won't heal a schema. You need to practice new thoughts, behaviors, and emotional responses repeatedly until they become natural.

Be patient with yourself. These schemas took years to form. They won't disappear in weeks. Most people need at least a year of consistent work to see significant change.

Get support. While you can do some of this work on your own, having a schema therapist makes it more effective and safer, especially for severe schemas or trauma.

Your Healing Plan

Here's how to start:

This week:

1. Choose one schema to focus on
2. Start a mode journal—track when the schema gets activated
3. Write out Healthy Adult responses to schema thoughts
4. Identify one behavior you could change

This month:

1. Make flash cards for your main schema
2. Try one imagery exercise with a mild memory
3. Do one behavioral experiment (break one schema-driven pattern)
4. Notice when modes shift and practice labeling them

This year:

1. Work through cognitive techniques for all your main schemas
2. Do deeper experiential work, ideally with a therapist
3. Practice new behaviors consistently
4. Build a stronger Healthy Adult mode
5. Connect with your Happy Child mode

You have the tools now. The question is: will you use them?

Healing requires courage. You have to face what you've been avoiding, feel what you've been numbing, and change what's familiar. It's not easy.

But it's possible. And it's worth it.

In the next chapter, we'll look at how to put all this together in your daily life—how to handle schema triggers in relationships, work, and real-world situations.

You're not just learning theory anymore. You're becoming someone different. Someone freer. Someone more whole.

Keep going.

Chapter 7: Putting It All Together

Healing Your Schemas in Real Life

You understand schemas now. You know about modes and coping styles. You've learned techniques for healing. But how does all this actually work in real life, when you're triggered at work, fighting with your partner, or lying awake at 3am with anxiety?

This chapter is about integration—taking everything you've learned and using it when it matters most, in the messy reality of daily life.

Creating Your Personal Schema Map

Before we get into specific situations, let's create your personal schema map. This is your guide to understanding your patterns.

Get your notebook and answer these questions:

Your Core Schemas: Which schemas do you have? List them in order of strength.

Example: "1. Abandonment (very strong), 2. Defectiveness (strong), 3. Failure (moderate), 4. Self-sacrifice (moderate)"

Your Triggers: What situations activate each schema?

Example: "Abandonment gets triggered when: my partner seems distant, someone cancels plans, I'm left alone unexpectedly, people take a long time to respond to messages"

Your Modes: Which modes do you go into when triggered?

Example: "Abandonment trigger → Vulnerable Child (panic, desperate) → Punitive Parent (you're too needy) → either Compliant Surrenderer (accept it and suffer) or Overcompensator (get controlling and angry)"

Your Coping Patterns: What do you do when schemas activate?

Example: "I send multiple texts, pick fights, withdraw emotionally, drink to numb the feelings, check social media compulsively"

Your Early Experiences: Where did these schemas come from?

Example: "Father left when I was six, never maintained contact. Mother was depressed and emotionally unavailable. Grew up feeling alone and unimportant."

Your Schema Map Example - Tyler:

Tyler created this map in therapy:

Primary Schema: Abandonment/Instability **Trigger Situations:** Partner pulling away, friends not responding, plans getting canceled, being alone **Mode Sequence:** Vulnerable Child (panic, terror) → Angry Child (rage at being abandoned) → Overcompensator (leave them first, be in control) **Behaviors:** End relationships prematurely, pick fights, test people constantly, refuse to get attached **Origins:** Mother had bipolar disorder, would be loving some weeks and gone other weeks, never knew what to expect **Impact:** Can't maintain relationships, lonely despite not wanting to be

Having this map helped Tyler understand himself. When he felt panic after his girlfriend didn't call one evening, he could think: "This is my abandonment schema. I'm in Vulnerable Child mode. The intensity of my fear is about my mother, not about this situation. I need to access my Healthy Adult instead of going into Overcompensator and ending this relationship."

Schema Work in Relationships

Relationships are where schemas come alive. The people closest to you will trigger your schemas more than anyone else. That's not their fault—that's how attachment works.

Let's look at how to handle common schema situations in relationships.

Situation 1: When Your Schema Gets Triggered

The scenario:

Inez and her boyfriend were having a good evening until he mentioned he was going out with friends on Saturday. Inez's abandonment schema immediately activated. She felt panicky and angry. Her old pattern would be to pick a fight or become clingy.

The schema-informed response:

Step 1 - Notice and Name Inez felt the familiar tightness in her chest and the urge to say something critical. She recognized it: "My abandonment schema just got triggered. I'm going into Vulnerable Child mode."

Step 2 - Pause Instead of immediately reacting, Inez said, "I need a minute." She went to the bathroom and did three deep breaths.

Step 3 - Reality Check She asked herself Healthy Adult questions:

- "Is this actually abandonment, or is it normal independence?"
- "What's the evidence he's pulling away versus just having a life?"
- "What would a secure person do in this situation?"

Step 4 - Self-Soothe She talked to her Vulnerable Child: "I know you're scared. This feels like when Mom would leave for days. But he's not Mom. He's going out for one evening. That's healthy. You're safe."

Step 5 - Respond from Healthy Adult Inez came back and said, "I noticed I had a reaction to that. My abandonment stuff got triggered. It's not rational, but I wanted to tell you what was happening instead of acting on it. Have fun with your friends on Saturday."

Her boyfriend appreciated her honesty. They talked briefly about her trigger, he reassured her, and the evening continued peacefully.

What this looks like for different schemas:

Defectiveness schema: Your partner makes a minor criticism.

- *Schema reaction:* "They see how defective I am. They're going to leave."
- *Healthy Adult response:* "This is one piece of feedback on one behavior. It doesn't mean I'm fundamentally flawed. I can hear this without feeling worthless."

Subjugation schema: Your partner asks you where you want to go for dinner.

- *Schema reaction:* Panic, "I don't know, whatever you want" (can't access own preferences)
- *Healthy Adult response:* "Let me take a minute to check in with myself. I think I want Thai food tonight."

Unrelenting standards schema: Your partner wants to relax and watch TV instead of being productive.

- *Schema reaction:* Judgment and irritation—"We should be doing something useful"
- *Healthy Adult response:* "My Demanding Parent is activated. Relaxing is actually healthy. I can let go of productivity for one evening."

Situation 2: When You Need to Communicate About Your Schemas

At some point, you'll want to explain your schemas to your partner. This helps them understand your reactions and support you better.

How to do it:

Pick a calm moment, not right after a trigger. Say something like:

"I want to tell you about something I'm working on. I have this pattern from my childhood [explain briefly]. Sometimes it gets activated and I react strongly. It's not about you—it's about old wounds. Here's what it looks like [describe symptoms]. Here's what would help [explain what you need]. Can we talk about how to handle this together?"

Example:

Felicity told her husband: "I'm working on my failure schema in therapy. I grew up with parents who were impossible to please, so I internalized this belief that I'm not good enough. When you give me feedback or criticism, even constructive stuff, my schema gets triggered and I either shut down or get defensive. I'm working on it, but it would help if you could be patient and maybe reassure me that one critique doesn't mean you think I'm a failure. Can you do that?"

Her husband was relieved to understand what was happening and happy to help.

Situation 3: When Your Partner Triggers Your Schema (But It's Actually Their Issue)

Sometimes what feels like your schema is actually your partner's problematic behavior. This is important to distinguish.

The key question: "Is my reaction proportional to what's happening, or am I overreacting due to my schema?"

Overreaction due to schema: Your partner is twenty minutes late. You feel abandoned, panicky, convinced they're leaving you. (That's schema—twenty minutes late is not abandonment.)

Appropriate reaction to real problem: Your partner is consistently hours late, doesn't call, and dismisses your feelings when you bring it up. You feel disrespected and hurt. (That's a real problem, not just schema.)

Another example:

Schema overreaction: Your partner mentions your friend is attractive. You feel crushed and defective, like you're not good enough. (That's defectiveness schema—noticing someone is attractive doesn't mean you're inadequate.)

Real problem: Your partner constantly compares you unfavorably to others, criticizes your appearance, and makes you feel bad about yourself. (That's actual mistreatment, not schema.)

The tricky part: Sometimes it's both. Your partner does something mildly problematic, and your schema makes your reaction much bigger.

Colette's boyfriend was sometimes dismissive when she was upset. This was a real issue—he needed to work on empathy. But Colette's emotional deprivation schema made her reaction extreme. She'd feel completely alone and unloved, spiral into depression for days, and question the entire relationship.

The solution? Colette needed to:

1. Work on her schema so her reaction was more proportional
2. Ask her boyfriend to work on his dismissiveness
3. Recognize that some dismissiveness doesn't mean total emotional deprivation

Both things were true: her schema was oversensitive, and he needed to do better.

Situation 4: Choosing Partners Differently

Once you understand your schemas, you'll notice you've been choosing partners who confirm them. People with abandonment schemas pick unavailable people. People with defectiveness schemas pick critical people. People with subjugation schemas pick controlling people.

This isn't conscious—it's what feels familiar.

Breaking the pattern:

Quentin had always dated women who were emotionally unavailable. He'd chase them, try to win them over, feel anxious constantly. This confirmed his abandonment and defectiveness schemas.

In therapy, he realized: "Unavailable women feel exciting because the anxiety feels like love. But actually, anxiety isn't love. It's just familiar."

He started dating someone different—someone who was available, consistent, and interested. At first, it felt boring. His schemas kept telling him: "This is too easy. Something must be wrong with her. This isn't real."

But Quentin pushed through the discomfort. He stayed with this woman even though his schemas screamed at him to run. After a few months, boring started feeling like security. Easy started feeling like healthy. He was retraining his nervous system to recognize safety.

Questions to ask when choosing partners:

- "Am I attracted to them, or am I attracted to the familiar pattern?"
- "Do they treat me well, or am I trying to earn their love?"
- "Do I feel anxious all the time, or do I feel secure?"
- "Would I want my best friend to date someone like this?"

If someone confirms your schemas—makes you feel abandoned, defective, controlled, or invisible—they're probably not the right person, no matter how strong the chemistry.

Schema Work at Work

Your workplace is another arena where schemas get triggered constantly. Bosses, colleagues, performance reviews, deadlines, competition—all of these can activate old patterns.

Common Work-Related Schema Triggers:

Failure schema: Performance reviews, mistakes, comparisons to colleagues, challenging projects **Unrelenting standards:** Never feeling work is good enough, working excessive hours, can't delegate **Subjugation:** Can't say no to extra work, don't advocate for yourself, let others take credit **Defectiveness:** Imposter syndrome, fear of being exposed as incompetent **Mistrust:** Can't trust colleagues, assume people are undermining you

Let's look at specific scenarios:

Scenario 1: Receiving Critical Feedback

The situation:

Andre's manager gave him feedback that his report needed more detail. Andre's failure and defectiveness schemas immediately activated. He felt crushing shame and was convinced he'd be fired.

The schema trap:

Old Andre would have:

- Spiraled into depression
- Avoided his manager out of shame
- Either worked obsessively to overcompensate or avoided the project altogether
- Beaten himself up with Punitive Parent attacks

The Healthy Adult response:

Step 1: Andre noticed his reaction was disproportionate: "My schemas are activated. This feedback doesn't mean I'm a failure or incompetent. It means one report needs more detail."

Step 2: He separated the facts from the schema story:

- **Fact:** Manager wants more detail in this report

- **Schema story:** "I'm incompetent and will be fired"
- **Reality:** This is normal feedback that I can address

Step 3: He responded professionally: "Thanks for the feedback. I'll add more detail to section three and send you an updated version by Friday. Any other specific areas you'd like me to expand?"

Step 4: He soothed his Vulnerable Child later: "That felt scary because it reminded you of Dad saying nothing you did was good enough. But your manager isn't Dad. This is just work feedback. You're doing fine."

Scenario 2: Setting Boundaries

The situation:

Dana's colleague kept asking her to cover his shifts. Dana had self-sacrifice and subjugation schemas. She'd always said yes, even when exhausted, because saying no felt impossible.

The schema trap:

Dana believed:

- Other people's needs matter more than hers
- Saying no is selfish
- People will be angry if she doesn't help
- Her worth comes from being helpful

The Healthy Adult response:

Dana practiced with her therapist: "I can't cover your shift this time. I have plans." She didn't need to justify or over-explain.

The first time she said no, she felt crushing guilt. Her Punitive Parent attacked: "You're so selfish. What kind of person won't help a colleague?"

But Dana's Healthy Adult fought back: "I'm not selfish for having boundaries. I've covered his shifts six times. He can find someone else. My plans matter too."

Her colleague said "Okay, no problem" and asked someone else.

Dana survived saying no. The guilt decreased each time she practiced.

Scenario 3: Dealing With Success

Ironically, success can trigger schemas as much as failure.

The situation:

Georgina got promoted. Most people would be thrilled, but Georgina's defectiveness schema immediately activated. She thought: "They made a mistake promoting me. Eventually they'll see I'm not qualified. I'm a fraud."

The schema trap:

Georgina almost turned down the promotion. Her schema told her she'd fail, be exposed as incompetent, and humiliate herself.

The Healthy Adult response:

Georgina recognized this was imposter syndrome—a classic defectiveness schema reaction.

She gathered evidence:

- She'd been successful in her current role for three years
- Her performance reviews were consistently excellent
- Her colleagues respected her work
- She'd led projects that went well
- She had the skills needed for the new role

She told her therapist: "My schema is terrified of being exposed. But that's the child who was told she was stupid, not reality. I'm qualified for this promotion."

She accepted the role. Yes, she felt anxious. But she pushed through the schema's predictions and succeeded.

Schema Work in Friendships

Friendships can trigger schemas too, especially abandonment, social isolation, and defectiveness schemas.

The Schema Challenge:

Pauline's friend group made plans without inviting her. Her social isolation and defectiveness schemas exploded: "They don't really like me. I don't belong. They probably just tolerate me."

Old response: Pull away from the friendship, assume she's not wanted, isolate herself

Healthy Adult response:

Pauline sat with the discomfort and checked: "Is this schema, or is this real?"

She looked at evidence:

- These friends had included her in many plans
- They called her when upset and wanted support
- They'd celebrated her birthday enthusiastically last month
- They'd invited her to previous events

She decided to ask directly instead of assuming: "Hey, I noticed you guys made plans for Saturday. I'm feeling a bit left out—was there a reason I wasn't included?"

Turns out, they'd assumed she was busy because she'd been traveling. They apologized and invited her to the next thing.

By checking reality instead of accepting her schema's story, Pauline saved the friendship.

Schema Work in Parenting

If you have children, you absolutely must work on your schemas. Otherwise, you'll pass them on.

This isn't about being a perfect parent—that's impossible. It's about not recreating your childhood wounds in your kids.

Common Schema-Driven Parenting Mistakes:

Abandonment schema: Being overprotective, not letting kids have independence, creating enmeshment

Defectiveness schema: Being overly critical (unconsciously trying to help them avoid your mistakes), or being permissive (wanting them to feel better than you did)

Failure schema: Pushing kids too hard to achieve, living through their success

Emotional deprivation: Being emotionally distant with your own kids, not knowing how to nurture

Unrelenting standards: Demanding perfection, conditional love based on achievement

Example:

Rodrigo had unrelenting standards and failure schemas from his hypercritical father. He found himself doing the same thing to his son—nothing was ever good enough, he'd focus on mistakes instead of effort.

After starting schema therapy, Rodrigo caught himself mid-criticism: "Wait. This is my Demanding Parent talking. This is what my father did to me. I don't want to pass this on."

He stopped, took a breath, and said to his son: "Actually, you worked really hard on this project. I'm proud of your effort. That's what matters."

His son's face lit up. Rodrigo realized: "I can break this cycle. I can be the parent I needed."

Real-Life Transformations: Before and After

Let's look at three people who did the work and how their lives changed:

Transformation 1: Rachel

Before:

- Strong abandonment schema
- Coped by being clingy and testing partners
- Went through relationships quickly—would panic and push people away
- Felt lonely and convinced she'd end up alone
- In Vulnerable Child mode most of the time

The Work:

- Two years of schema therapy
- Imagery rescripting of abandonment experiences
- Learning to tolerate normal distance
- Not texting immediately when anxious
- Choosing a stable partner instead of exciting but unavailable ones
- Building Healthy Adult mode

After:

- In a stable relationship for three years
- Can handle partner going away for work without panic
- Catches abandonment schema early: "Oh, that's just my fear talking"

- Still gets triggered sometimes, but recovers quickly
- Mostly in Healthy Adult mode, with occasional Vulnerable Child moments she can soothe

Rachel's insight: "I used to think relationships were supposed to feel anxious and intense. Now I know that was just my schema. Real love feels safe. It took time to adjust to that, but now I can't imagine going back."

Transformation 2: David

Before:

- Failure and defectiveness schemas
- Coped by avoiding challenges and underachieving
- Working a job below his capabilities
- Depressed and stuck
- In Detached Protector mode often

The Work:

- Individual therapy with schema focus
- Cognitive work on evidence of competence
- Behavioral experiments—taking on small challenges
- Processing shame from childhood experiences
- Building self-compassion
- Gradually increasing challenge level

After:

- Started his own business after two years of healing work
- Takes on challenges even when scared
- When he makes mistakes: "That's learning, not failure"
- Still has moments of doubt but doesn't let them stop him
- Mostly in Healthy Adult mode with occasional Vulnerable Child moments

David's insight: "I realized I'd been living my father's voice in my head: 'You'll never amount to anything.' Once I understood that was his shame, not my reality, I could start building my actual life. I'm not perfect, but I'm done letting fear stop me."

Transformation 3: Maya

Before:

- Self-sacrifice and subjugation schemas
- Coped by compulsively taking care of everyone else
- Couldn't say no, set boundaries, or prioritize herself
- Resentful and exhausted
- In Compliant Surrenderer mode constantly

The Work:

- Schema therapy plus boundaries work
- Learning to identify her own needs
- Practicing saying no in small situations
- Empty chair work expressing anger at family
- Self-compassion exercises
- Accepting guilt as part of healing

After:

- Can say no without excessive guilt
- Takes time for herself without feeling selfish
- Left a draining friendship that was one-sided
- Has energy because she's not overextended
- Helps people by choice, not compulsion
- Mostly in Healthy Adult mode

Maya's insight: "The hardest part was accepting that some people got angry when I set boundaries. My schema said that was proof I was selfish. But my therapist helped me see: people who benefited from my lack of boundaries would resist change. That's about them, not me. Real friends adjusted and respected my needs."

Your Action Plan for Real-Life Schema Work

Here's your roadmap for applying schema work to your life:

Week 1: Tracking

- Use your schema map to identify triggers throughout the week
- Notice patterns: What situations activate which schemas?
- Don't try to change anything yet—just observe and learn

Week 2-4: Small Interventions

- Pick one recurring situation (example: Sunday dinner with critical family)
- Plan ahead: "When my mother criticizes me, I'll recognize it's my defectiveness schema, I won't engage defensively, I'll use my Healthy Adult response"
- Practice in low-stakes situations first
- Review what worked and what didn't

Month 2: Relationship Focus

- Talk to your partner about one main schema
- Practice pausing when triggered instead of reacting
- Use "I'm having a schema reaction" language
- Ask for what you need: reassurance, space, understanding

Month 3: Work Focus

- Identify your main work-related schema pattern
- Experiment with one new behavior (saying no, taking on a challenge, asking for feedback)
- Notice how your schema predicts disaster that doesn't happen
- Build evidence that contradicts your schema

Month 4-6: Deeper Work

- Continue practicing all the above
- Add experiential techniques if you're ready

- Notice shifts in how quickly you recover from triggers
- Celebrate progress, even small wins

Month 6-12: Integration

- Schema awareness becomes more automatic
- Healthy Adult mode gets stronger and more accessible
- You catch yourself earlier in the schema cycle
- Recovery time decreases
- Old patterns still emerge but have less power

Year 2+: Maintenance

- Schemas don't disappear, but they weaken significantly
- You know your patterns so well you can often interrupt them before they fully activate
- Healthy Adult is your default most of the time
- You're teaching others (partners, kids, friends) about healthy patterns

Common Challenges and How to Handle Them

Challenge 1: "I keep forgetting to use these tools when I'm triggered"

This is normal. When schemas activate, they hijack your brain. You don't think clearly.

Solution:

- Create visual reminders (notes on your phone, cards in your wallet)
- Practice when calm so tools become more automatic
- Review triggers at the end of each day and think through what you could have done differently
- Be patient—this takes hundreds of repetitions

Challenge 2: "I'm doing everything right but still feel bad"

Healing takes time. You might be doing all the cognitive work and still feel the emotional pull of the schema.

Solution:

- Add experiential techniques—thinking alone isn't enough
- Allow yourself to feel the feelings while also knowing they'll pass
- Remember: you can feel bad and still make healthy choices
- Measure progress by behavior changes, not just feelings

Challenge 3: "My partner/family isn't supporting this work"

Some people in your life benefited from your schemas. They might resist your changes.

Solution:

- Keep doing the work anyway—you don't need permission
- Find support elsewhere (therapist, friends, support groups)
- Accept that some relationships might end or change as you heal
- Remember: people who truly love you will eventually support your growth

Challenge 4: "I feel like I'm taking two steps forward, one step back"

That's exactly what healing looks like. It's not linear.

Solution:

- Track overall trends, not daily fluctuations
- Expect setbacks after stress or triggers
- See setbacks as information, not failure
- Compare yourself to six months ago, not yesterday

Final Encouragement

Healing schemas in real life is messy. You'll have moments of clarity and moments of total regression. You'll catch yourself mid-pattern sometimes and completely miss it other times. You'll make progress and then get triggered back to old behaviors.

All of that is normal. All of that is part of the process.

What matters is that you keep showing up. You keep noticing. You keep trying.

Three months from now, look back at this moment. You'll see changes you can't perceive today. Six months from now, patterns that feel impossible to break will have loosened. A year from now, you'll have moments where you think: "I handled that completely differently than I would have before."

You're not trying to be perfect. You're trying to be a little bit healthier, a little bit more aware, a little bit more yourself.

That's enough. That's everything.

In the next chapter, we'll talk about maintaining these changes long-term and what life looks like when you're living more from your Healthy Adult than your schemas.

You're almost there. Keep going.

Chapter 8: Living Your New Story

You've done the work. You've identified your schemas, understood where they came from, learned the techniques, and started applying them to your life. You're not the same person who started this book.

But here's the question: how do you maintain these changes? How do you keep growing? And what does life actually look like when you're not controlled by your schemas anymore?

This chapter is about the long game—living your new story for the rest of your life.

Understanding That Schemas Don't Disappear

Let me be honest with you about something important: your schemas will never completely disappear.

I know that's not what you wanted to hear. You wanted me to say that if you do the work, the schemas will vanish and you'll be free forever.

But that's not how it works.

Your schemas were formed during crucial developmental periods. They're wired into your nervous system. They're part of your history, your story, your journey.

What changes isn't whether you have schemas. What changes is:

How often they get triggered (less frequently as you heal) **How intensely you experience them** (less overwhelming over time) **How long they last** (you recover faster) **How much control they have** (your Healthy Adult gets stronger) **How you respond to them** (with compassion, not panic)

Think of it like this: Imagine you grew up in a house with a faulty smoke detector that went off constantly, even when there was no fire. Your nervous system learned to panic every time you smelled anything burning.

Even after you move out and live in a safe house with a working detector, the smell of something burning might still trigger that panic response. Your body remembers.

But now you can catch it: "Oh, that's just my old pattern. There's no fire. I'm safe." The panic might show up, but you don't have to let it run your life.

That's what healing looks like.

The Stages of Schema Recovery

Most people go through predictable stages as they heal. Knowing what to expect helps you recognize progress.

Stage 1: Awareness (Months 1-3)

What's happening: You're learning about schemas, identifying yours, connecting dots between past and present.

What it feels like: Sometimes relieving ("Oh, that's why I do that!"), sometimes overwhelming (there's so much to work on), often emotional (childhood pain surfaces).

Your main job: Observe and learn. Don't try to change everything yet. Just notice patterns.

Liam's experience: "In the first few months, I felt like someone turned on a light in a room I'd been sitting in the dark. I started seeing my abandonment schema everywhere—in every relationship, every anxiety, every behavior. It was a lot, but also such a relief to understand."

Stage 2: Experimentation (Months 3-6)

What's happening: You're trying new responses, testing new behaviors, practicing techniques.

What it feels like: Awkward, uncomfortable, sometimes like you're faking it. Lots of two-steps-forward-one-step-back moments.

Your main job: Practice, even when it feels unnatural. Build new neural pathways through repetition.

Nina's experience: "I started saying no to things, and it felt terrible. Like I was being mean. My whole body screamed at me to apologize and take it back. But I pushed through. Each time I survived saying no, it got a tiny bit easier."

Stage 3: Integration (Months 6-12)

What's happening: New responses start feeling more natural. Your Healthy Adult is getting stronger. You catch schemas earlier in the cycle.

What it feels like: Cautiously optimistic. You notice real changes but still have significant struggles. Progress feels uneven.

Your main job: Keep practicing. Trust the process even when you have setbacks.

Ivan's experience: "Around month eight, I had this moment where my boss criticized something and instead of spiraling into shame, I just... took the feedback and moved on. It wasn't until later that I realized: I didn't have a schema reaction. My Healthy Adult just handled it. That's when I knew something was really changing."

Stage 4: Consolidation (Years 1-2)

What's happening: Changes feel more solid. Schemas still get triggered but you recover quickly. Healthy Adult is your default most of the time.

What it feels like: Lighter, freer, more yourself. Occasional schema triggers feel more like brief clouds passing through rather than storms that destroy everything.

Your main job: Maintain your gains. Continue practicing. Stay aware of triggers.

Claudia's experience: "After about eighteen months, I realized I'd gone three weeks without a major abandonment panic. Three weeks! That used to be impossible. I still had moments of anxiety, but they didn't take over anymore. I was living instead of just surviving."

Stage 5: Maintenance (Year 2+)

What's happening: You've built a new baseline. Schemas are manageable. You have tools that work. Life feels qualitatively different.

What it feels like: Like you're living your actual life, not just reacting to old wounds. Schemas are background noise, not the main event.

Your main job: Stay vigilant during high-stress periods. Keep growing. Pass it on.

Kirk's experience: "I'm five years into this work now. I still have my failure schema—it shows up when I'm stressed or trying something new. But it's like an old friend I know how to manage rather than a monster that controls me. I catch it, talk to it, and move forward. That's the difference."

Building Resilience: Preventing Schema Relapses

Schemas get stronger during stress, major life changes, or when you're tired, sick, or overwhelmed. You need strategies to maintain your gains during difficult periods.

High-Risk Situations for Schema Relapse:

Major life stress:

- Job loss or major work changes
- Relationship breakup or marriage difficulties
- Health crisis (yours or a loved one's)
- Financial problems
- Moving, especially to a new city
- Loss of a loved one

Emotional states:

- Depression
- Anxiety or panic
- Physical exhaustion
- Hunger (yes, really—being "hangry" weakens Healthy Adult)
- Sleep deprivation
- Illness

Relationship dynamics:

- New relationship (attachment fears surge)
- Partner pulling away or acting distant
- Conflict or criticism
- Betrayal or rejection
- Someone leaving

When Jasmine's story:

Jasmine had worked on her defectiveness schema for two years. She was doing well—confident at work, in a healthy relationship, feeling good about herself.

Then she got laid off.

Immediately, her defectiveness schema came roaring back: "See? You're not good enough. They got rid of you. Everyone will see you're a fraud."

All her progress felt like it had vanished overnight.

What helped Jasmine:

1. She recognized what was happening: "This is a schema flare-up due to stress, not truth. The schema is louder right now, but that doesn't mean all my healing disappeared."

2. She went back to basics: Daily flash cards, mode journaling, regular therapy sessions, reaching out to supportive friends.

3. She gave herself compassion: "Of course my schema is activated. I'm stressed and scared. That's normal. I don't need to beat myself up for having old feelings."

4. She remembered evidence: "I felt this way before and survived. I have skills now that I didn't have two years ago. I can get through this."

After three months, Jasmine found a new job. Her schema settled back down. She'd weathered the storm without completely regressing.

Your Relapse Prevention Plan

Create this plan now, while you're doing okay, so you have it when things get hard.

My warning signs that schemas are taking over:

- I'm isolating more than usual
- I'm having trouble sleeping
- I'm more irritable or emotional
- I'm avoiding responsibilities
- I'm returning to old coping behaviors (drinking, overeating, overworking, etc.)

My high-risk triggers:

- Conflict with partner
- Work criticism
- Being alone for extended periods
- Family gatherings
- Anniversary dates of losses

My coping plan when triggered:

1. Call my therapist or a supportive friend
2. Review my flash cards and schema map
3. Journal about what's happening
4. Do one thing that nurtures me each day
5. Don't make major decisions until I'm calmer
6. Remind myself: "This is temporary. I have skills. I can handle this."

My support team:

- Therapist: [name and contact]
- Supportive friends: [names]
- Family members who understand: [names]
- Support group or online community: [resource]

Deepening the Work: Advanced Schema Healing

After you've been doing basic schema work for a while, you can go deeper.

Working With Positive Schemas

So far, we've focused on healing maladaptive schemas. But you can also build positive schemas—healthy beliefs about yourself and the world.

Examples of positive schemas:

- "I'm worthy of love and belonging"
- "I'm capable and competent"
- "I can handle challenges"

- "My needs matter"
- "I'm safe in healthy relationships"
- "The world is generally good, though not perfect"

How to build them:

1. Gather evidence actively Keep a "positive schema journal." Every day, write down evidence for your positive schema.

Example: If you're building "I'm competent," you might write:

- "Fixed the printer at work"
- "Figured out that complex recipe"
- "Helped my friend troubleshoot their computer"
- "Managed my budget well this month"

2. Create positive imagery Use the imagery rescripting technique, but instead of revisiting painful memories, create new positive ones.

Imagine yourself as a child receiving what you needed. See adult you giving young you love, protection, encouragement. Make it vivid and emotional.

3. Act as if the positive schema is true Even when you don't fully believe it, act from the positive schema. Over time, your belief will catch up to your behavior.

If your positive schema is "I'm worthy of love," act like someone who believes that: set boundaries, expect respect, walk away from mistreatment.

Shadow Work: Integrating Rejected Parts

Sometimes we develop schemas not just from what happened to us, but from parts of ourselves we had to reject to survive.

Maybe you had to suppress your anger to stay safe. Maybe you had to hide your creativity to fit in. Maybe you had to deny your needs to get conditional love.

These rejected parts don't disappear—they go into shadow, influencing you unconsciously.

Camilla's shadow work:

Camilla grew up in a family where showing any selfishness was forbidden. She developed an extreme self-sacrifice schema. But underneath, she had normal desires and needs she'd learned to suppress.

In therapy, she did shadow work—reclaiming her right to have needs, to say no, to be "selfish" sometimes. This felt dangerous at first. Her whole identity was built on being selfless.

But as she integrated this rejected part, she became more whole. She could be generous when she chose, not compulsively. She could ask for things without guilt. She could be selfish sometimes without feeling like a terrible person.

The rejected part needed welcome, not more rejection.

Your shadow work questions:

- What parts of myself did I learn were unacceptable?
- What emotions or needs did I have to suppress?
- What aspects of myself am I still rejecting?
- What would happen if I welcomed those parts back?

Teaching Schema Awareness to Your Children

If you have kids, one of the most powerful gifts you can give them is schema awareness at an age-appropriate level.

You're not going to sit a five-year-old down and explain early maladaptive schemas. But you can teach concepts that prevent schema formation.

For Young Children (Ages 3-7):

Teach emotional literacy: "You're feeling angry right now. Anger is okay. Let's figure out what you need."

Validate all emotions: "I see you're sad. Sad feelings are okay. Come here, let me hold you."

Model Healthy Adult responses: When you make mistakes: "Oops, I messed up. That's okay, I'll fix it. Everyone makes mistakes."

Separate behavior from identity: Not: "You're bad!" Instead: "You made a choice that hurt someone. That choice was not okay, but you're still a good kid. Let's figure out how to do better."

For Older Children (Ages 8-12):

Introduce the concept of "old stories": "Sometimes our brains tell us stories that aren't true. Like, 'I'm not good at math.' But that's just an old story. Let's challenge it."

Teach them about triggers: "Have you noticed that you get really upset when someone leaves you out? That's touching an old hurt. Let's talk about it."

Help them identify patterns: "I notice you avoid trying new things. What are you worried will happen?"

Model self-compassion: Let them see you being kind to yourself when you mess up.

For Teens (Ages 13+):

Introduce schema concepts explicitly: "Have you learned about schemas? They're patterns we develop from early experiences that affect how we see ourselves."

Help them identify their developing schemas: "It sounds like you might be developing a belief that people will reject you. Let's look at the evidence for and against that."

Teach them Healthy Adult skills: "When you're anxious, what could you tell yourself that would help?"

Normalize therapy and emotional work: "Lots of people do therapy. It's like having a coach for your emotional life."

The Ripple Effect: How Your Healing Helps Others

Here's something beautiful: when you heal your schemas, everyone around you benefits.

Your partner doesn't have to walk on eggshells or manage your triggers anymore. **Your children** grow up with a healthier model of emotional regulation. **Your friends** experience a more authentic, present version of you. **Your colleagues** work with someone more balanced and functional. **You** can show up fully in your own life.

And sometimes, your healing inspires others to start their own journey.

Monica's ripple effect:

Monica worked on her abandonment and self-sacrifice schemas for three years. She became less clingy, less afraid, more able to set boundaries.

Her sister watched this transformation and said, "I think I need to work on that stuff too. You seem so much happier."

Her teenage daughter, seeing Monica set boundaries, learned she could do the same: "If Mom can say no, maybe I can too."

Her best friend, supported through her healing journey, later went to therapy herself: "Watching you do this work made me realize I could too."

One person's healing creates possibility for others.

What Life Looks Like After Schema Work

Let me paint you a picture of what life can look like when you're not controlled by schemas anymore.

You still have bad days, but they don't destroy you.

You still have old patterns show up, but you catch them faster.

You still feel vulnerable sometimes, but you know how to comfort yourself.

You can tolerate discomfort without needing to escape it immediately.

You can sit with uncertainty without spiraling into panic.

You can receive love without waiting for it to be taken away.

You can try new things without assuming you'll fail.

You can make mistakes without feeling worthless.

You can ask for what you need without guilt or fear.

You can be alone without feeling abandoned.

You can be close to people without losing yourself.

You can handle criticism without crumbling.

You can celebrate success without waiting for disaster.

You can rest without feeling lazy.

You can say no without being cruel.

You can say yes without resentment.

You can be angry without being destructive.

You can be sad without being depressed.

You can be yourself without apologizing.

That's what freedom feels like.

Your New Story

You started this book with an old story—schemas formed in childhood that defined how you saw yourself and the world.

Now you have a choice: keep living that old story, or write a new one.

The new story doesn't erase the old one. Your past still happened. The wounds were real. The pain was real.

But in the new story, you're not defined by those wounds. You're defined by how you healed them.

In the old story, you were the abandoned child, the defective one, the failure, the invisible one.

In the new story, you're the one who survived, who did the work, who chose healing, who broke the cycle.

What's your new story?

Maybe it's: "I grew up feeling unlovable, and I spent years pushing people away to protect myself. But I learned that my fear was about the past, not the present. I learned to let people in. Now I have real connections, and I'm not afraid of love anymore."

Or: "I grew up believing I was incompetent, and I played small my whole life. But I learned that my capabilities were always there—I just couldn't see them. I learned to try things even when I'm scared. Now I'm building a life I'm proud of."

Or: "I grew up thinking my needs didn't matter, and I spent decades taking care of everyone else. But I learned that I matter too. I learned to set boundaries and take care of myself. Now I can give to others from fullness, not from emptiness."

Write your new story. Say it out loud. Believe it into existence.

The Practice of Maintenance

To maintain your healing long-term, you need ongoing practices. Here are the ones that matter most:

Daily:

- Check in with yourself: "What mode am I in? What do I need right now?"
- Use flash cards or affirmations if schemas feel active
- Practice one small Healthy Adult choice

Weekly:

- Review triggers and responses from the week
- Journal about patterns you notice
- Do something that connects you with Happy Child (play, creativity, fun)

Monthly:

- Assess overall progress: "Am I better than I was a month ago?"
- Identify new areas to work on
- Read through your schema map and update it

Yearly:

- Do a full review: What's changed? What still needs work?
- Set new healing goals
- Celebrate your progress

During stress:

- Go back to basics: more therapy, more journaling, more self-care
- Reach out for support
- Remember: setbacks don't erase progress

When to Seek Professional Help

While you can do a lot of schema work on your own, some situations really require a therapist:

Seek professional help if:

- Your schemas involve severe trauma or abuse
- You're dealing with complex PTSD
- You have active self-harm or suicidal thoughts
- You're in an abusive relationship and can't see it
- Your schemas are so strong you can't function
- You're stuck and not making progress on your own
- You have severe addiction issues
- You need medication evaluation

A good schema therapist can:

- Provide the limited reparenting you need
- Guide you through deep experiential work safely
- Catch patterns you can't see yourself
- Hold hope when you feel hopeless
- Teach you techniques effectively
- Validate your experience

There's no shame in needing help. Therapy isn't weakness—it's wisdom.

Final Words: You're Not Done, and That's Okay

Here's the truth: you're never "done" with schema work. Healing isn't a destination—it's a practice, a way of life.

You'll be 80 years old and still occasionally catch your abandonment schema, your failure schema, your old patterns showing up.

And that's okay.

Because you'll also be 80 years old with decades of evidence that you can handle them. You'll have a lifetime of proof that your schemas aren't truth. You'll have accumulated so many memories of choosing differently that the old patterns will have very little power left.

The goal isn't perfection. The goal isn't to never have schema reactions.

The goal is to live more from your Healthy Adult than your wounded child. To catch patterns earlier. To recover faster. To hurt less. To love better. To be more free.

You're already doing that. Every time you read this book, every time you catch a schema mid-activation, every time you choose a Healthy Adult response instead of an old coping pattern—you're doing it.

You started this journey because something in your life wasn't working. You were stuck in patterns you couldn't break. You were hurting in ways you couldn't explain.

Now you understand. Now you have tools. Now you have hope.

The schemas that once controlled you? They're just old programs running. And you know how to interrupt them now.

The modes that used to take over? You can recognize and manage them now.

The coping styles that once felt necessary? You're replacing them with healthier options now.

This is what transformation looks like. Not perfect. Not painless. But real.

You're different than when you started. You know things now you didn't know before. You can do things now you couldn't do before. You're becoming who you were always meant to be—before the wounds, before the schemas, before the survival strategies.

That person was always there, waiting.

Welcome home.

Resources for Your Continued Journey

Books:

- "Reinventing Your Life" by Jeffrey Young and Janet Klosko
- "Schema Therapy: A Practitioner's Guide" by Jeffrey Young, Janet Klosko, and Marjorie Weishaar
- "The Body Keeps the Score" by Bessel van der Kolk
- "Complex PTSD: From Surviving to Thriving" by Pete Walker

Finding a Therapist:

- International Society of Schema Therapy (ISST): www.schematherapysociety.org
- Psychology Today therapist directory with schema therapy filter
- Ask potential therapists: "Are you trained in schema therapy?"

Online Resources:

- Schema therapy worksheets and handouts
- Schema therapy podcasts and videos
- Online schema therapy communities and support groups

Apps:

- Mood tracking apps to monitor schema triggers
- Meditation apps for emotion regulation

- Journaling apps for tracking patterns

Your Commitment

I want to ask you to make a commitment to yourself:

I commit to continuing this work. I commit to catching my schemas when they arise. I commit to being kind to myself when I struggle. I commit to choosing my Healthy Adult over my old patterns. I commit to healing, even when it's hard. I commit to my own freedom.

Sign your name:

_____

Date:

_____

Come back to this commitment when you want to give up. You made a promise to yourself. Keep it.

The End Is the Beginning

This is the end of the book, but it's just the beginning of your new story.

Everything you've learned here—the schemas, the modes, the techniques, the insights—is just the foundation. The real work happens in your life, every day, in every choice you make.

Some days you'll do great. Other days you'll feel like you learned nothing. Both are part of the journey.

The schema that brought you to this book—the one that convinced you something was wrong with you—was lying. You're not broken. You never were.

You're a person who experienced things that created patterns. Those patterns made sense at the time. They helped you survive.

Now you're ready to do more than survive. You're ready to live.

Go live.

With compassion for your wounded parts. With pride in your strength. With hope for your future. With faith in your ability to heal.

You've got this.

And when you doubt that—when your schemas tell you otherwise—come back to these pages. Remember what you've learned. Remember who you're becoming.

You're writing a new story now.

Make it a good one.

Appendix A: Schema Questionnaire for Self-Assessment

This questionnaire helps you identify which of the 18 early maladaptive schemas you might have. Read each statement and rate how true it feels for you most of the time.

Rating Scale: 1 = Completely untrue of me 2 = Mostly untrue of me 3 = Slightly more true than untrue 4 = Moderately true of me 5 = Mostly true of me 6 = Describes me perfectly

Important Notes:

- Answer based on how you typically feel, not just how you feel today

- Think about patterns across your life, not isolated incidents

- There are no right or wrong answers

- Be honest—this is for your eyes only

- If you score high on several items in a category, that schema is likely active for you

---

DOMAIN 1: DISCONNECTION AND REJECTION

Schema 1: Abandonment/Instability

_____ 1. I worry that people I feel close to will leave me or abandon me. _____ 2. I feel clingy because I'm afraid people will leave. _____ 3. I don't have a stable, reliable person who has always been there for me. _____ 4. I can't let myself get too attached because people never stay. _____ 5. When someone I love pulls away even slightly, I panic. _____ 6. I worry constantly about losing the people I care about. _____ 7. I test people to see if they'll stay with me. _____ 8. I feel desperate when I think someone might leave.

Total Score for Abandonment: _____ (32-48 = Very strong schema; 24-31 = Strong schema; 16-23 = Moderate schema; 8-15 = Mild or not present)

Schema 2: Mistrust/Abuse

_____ 1. I expect people to hurt, use, or take advantage of me. _____ 2. I'm constantly on guard, waiting for people to betray me. _____ 3. People have abused, humiliated, or manipulated me throughout my life. _____ 4. I don't trust anyone's motives—people always want something. _____ 5. I believe people are basically selfish and will hurt me if given the chance. _____ 6. I look for hidden agendas in people's nice behavior. _____ 7. I've been physically, emotionally, or sexually abused. _____ 8. I expect deception and lies from others.

Total Score for Mistrust/Abuse: _____

Schema 3: Emotional Deprivation

_____ 1. I feel like no one really understands me or cares about my feelings. _____ 2. I've never had someone who truly listens to me and cares about what I need. _____ 3. I feel emotionally empty and lonely, even around others. _____ 4. I don't expect emotional support or comfort from others. _____ 5. No one has really been there for me emotionally. _____ 6. I feel like my emotional needs don't matter to anyone. _____ 7. I've never felt genuinely nurtured or cared for. _____ 8. I don't bother sharing my feelings because no one cares anyway.

Total Score for Emotional Deprivation: _____

Schema 4: Defectiveness/Shame

_____ 1. I feel fundamentally flawed and unworthy of love. _____ 2. If people really knew me, they'd see how defective I am and reject me. _____ 3. I'm ashamed of who I am at my core. _____ 4. I hide my true self because I believe I'm not good enough. _____ 5. I feel different from others in some basic, defective way. _____ 6. No one could love me if they saw the real me. _____ 7. I'm constantly worried that my flaws will be exposed. _____ 8. I feel worthless and damaged inside.

Total Score for Defectiveness/Shame: _____

Schema 5: Social Isolation/Alienation

_____ 1. I feel different from other people, like I don't belong anywhere. _____ 2. I'm on the outside looking in—never truly part of any group. _____ 3. My family was different in ways that made me feel isolated. _____ 4. I don't fit in with other people. _____ 5. I feel like an outsider, even with people I know well. _____ 6. I watch others connect easily while I remain apart. _____ 7. No group or community feels like home to me. _____ 8. I'm fundamentally different in ways that separate me from others.

Total Score for Social Isolation: _____

DOMAIN 2: IMPAIRED AUTONOMY AND PERFORMANCE

Schema 6: Dependence/Incompetence

_____ 1. I don't feel capable of handling everyday life without help from others. _____ 2. I need others to help me make decisions, even simple ones. _____ 3. I can't trust my own judgment about daily matters. _____ 4. I feel helpless when faced with normal adult responsibilities. _____ 5. I depend on others to function in day-to-day life. _____ 6. I don't believe I can solve problems on my own. _____ 7. I need constant reassurance and advice from others. _____ 8. I feel like I can't survive without someone to help me.

Total Score for Dependence/Incompetence: _____

Schema 7: Vulnerability to Harm or Illness

_____ 1. I worry constantly that catastrophe will strike at any moment. _____ 2. I feel like I'm about to have a serious medical problem. _____ 3. I can't shake the feeling that something terrible is about to happen. _____ 4. I avoid situations I perceive as dangerous, even when others think they're safe. _____ 5. I'm hypervigilant about potential threats and disasters. _____ 6. I worry excessively about illness, financial ruin, or random disasters. _____ 7. I check locks, stoves, and other things repeatedly for safety. _____ 8. The world feels dangerous and unpredictable to me.

Total Score for Vulnerability: _____

Schema 8: Enmeshment/Undeveloped Self

_____ 1. I'm so close to certain people that I don't have my own identity. _____ 2. I can't make decisions without extensive input from someone close to me. _____ 3. I don't know who I am apart from certain important people in my life. _____ 4. I feel empty when I'm not extremely close to someone. _____ 5. I can't tell where my feelings end and another person's begin. _____ 6. I've never developed my own interests, opinions, or direction. _____ 7. I feel guilty when I try to separate or be independent. _____ 8. I lose myself completely in relationships.

Total Score for Enmeshment: _____

Schema 9: Failure

_____ 1. I believe I'm fundamentally inadequate compared to others. _____ 2. I'm convinced I'll fail at anything important I try. _____ 3. I'm less capable than most people in areas of work or achievement. _____ 4. I avoid challenges because I'm sure I'll fail. _____ 5. When I succeed, I attribute it to luck, not ability. _____ 6. I feel like a failure even when I'm doing okay objectively. _____ 7. I constantly compare myself to others and come up short. _____ 8. I believe I lack the intelligence or talent to succeed.

Total Score for Failure: ____

DOMAIN 3: IMPAIRED LIMITS

Schema 10: Entitlement/Grandiosity

____ 1. I should be able to do or have whatever I want, regardless of others. ____ 2. I have trouble accepting normal limits on my behavior. ____ 3. I feel superior to most people. ____ 4. Rules that apply to others shouldn't apply to me. ____ 5. I get angry when people don't do what I want or give me what I deserve. ____ 6. I have difficulty understanding or caring about others' perspectives. ____ 7. I believe my needs and desires are more important than others'. ____ 8. I expect special treatment or privileges.

Total Score for Entitlement: ____

Schema 11: Insufficient Self-Control/Self-Discipline

____ 1. I can't make myself do things I find boring or unpleasant. ____ 2. I give up easily when things get difficult. ____ 3. I act on impulses even when I know I shouldn't. ____ 4. I have trouble following through on commitments or completing tasks. ____ 5. I choose immediate pleasure over long-term goals. ____ 6. I can't delay gratification, even briefly. ____ 7. I struggle with basic self-discipline (diet, exercise, work, finances). ____ 8. I avoid discomfort at all costs, even when it would benefit me.

Total Score for Insufficient Self-Control: ____

DOMAIN 4: OTHER-DIRECTEDNESS

Schema 12: Subjugation

____ 1. I let others control me to avoid anger, retaliation, or abandonment. ____ 2. I suppress my feelings and needs to keep others happy. _____ 3. I feel trapped—like I have to give in to others' wishes. _____ 4. If I express my needs, something bad will happen. _____ 5. I go along with what others want, even when I strongly disagree. _____ 6. My opinions and desires don't matter as much as others'. _____ 7. I build up resentment because I can never express what I want. _____ 8. I feel controlled by others and can't assert myself.

Total Score for Subjugation: _____

Schema 13: Self-Sacrifice

_____ 1. I focus on meeting others' needs at the expense of my own. _____ 2. I feel selfish when I do things for myself. _____ 3. I'm so busy taking care of others that I neglect myself. _____ 4. I feel guilty when I'm not helping someone. _____ 5. I give to others compulsively, even when it hurts me. _____ 6. My purpose is to take care of others—my needs come last. _____ 7. I can't say no when people need help. _____ 8. I feel responsible for others' happiness and wellbeing.

Total Score for Self-Sacrifice: _____

Schema 14: Approval-Seeking/Recognition-Seeking

_____ 1. My self-esteem depends almost entirely on others' opinions of me. _____ 2. I need constant approval, attention, or recognition to feel okay. _____ 3. I make decisions based on what others will think, not what I want. _____ 4. I'm preoccupied with my image, status, or appearance. _____ 5. I can't enjoy success unless others recognize and admire it. _____ 6. I'm extremely sensitive to criticism or disapproval. _____ 7. I choose relationships, jobs, and activities based on how they look to others. _____ 8. I feel worthless when I don't get validation from others.

Total Score for Approval-Seeking: _____

DOMAIN 5: OVERVIGILANCE AND INHIBITION

Schema 15: Negativity/Pessimism

_____ 1. I expect things to go wrong, no matter how well they're going now. _____ 2. I focus on the negative aspects of situations and minimize the positive. _____ 3. I worry constantly about worst-case scenarios. _____ 4. I can't enjoy good things because I'm waiting for them to fall apart. _____ 5. When something good happens, I think "This won't last." _____ 6. I expect disappointment and prepare for bad outcomes. _____ 7. I'm pessimistic about my future. _____ 8. I notice problems more than I notice what's going well.

Total Score for Negativity/Pessimism: _____

Schema 16: Emotional Inhibition

_____ 1. I keep my emotions inside and don't express them. _____ 2. Showing feelings feels dangerous, embarrassing, or weak. _____ 3. I'm uncomfortable when others express strong emotions. _____ 4. I control my emotions tightly and appear stoic. _____ 5. Spontaneous emotional expression makes me very uncomfortable. _____ 6. I suppress feelings so much that I often don't know what I'm feeling. _____ 7. I was taught that showing emotion is inappropriate or weak. _____ 8. I have physical symptoms (headaches, tension, digestive issues) from suppressed feelings.

Total Score for Emotional Inhibition: _____

Schema 17: Unrelenting Standards/Hypercriticalness

_____ 1. I set impossibly high standards for myself. _____ 2. Nothing I do is ever good enough. _____ 3. I must be the best, or else I feel like a failure. _____ 4. I'm extremely critical of myself and others. _____ 5. I focus on efficiency, productivity, and achievement at the expense of happiness. _____ 6. I can't relax because there's always more to do.

_____ 7. Good enough is never good enough—things must be perfect.
_____ 8. I feel pressure constantly to meet high standards.

Total Score for Unrelenting Standards: _____

Schema 18: Punitiveness

_____ 1. I believe people should be severely punished for mistakes.
_____ 2. I'm extremely harsh and unforgiving toward myself when I mess up. _____ 3. I think people deserve to suffer when they do wrong.
_____ 4. I can't forgive myself or others easily. _____ 5. I punish myself (through self-denial, self-harm, or harsh self-criticism). _____ 6. I'm intolerant of human weakness or imperfection. _____ 7. When someone hurts me, I want them to suffer for it. _____ 8. I believe strict punishment is necessary for people to learn.

Total Score for Punitiveness: _____

INTERPRETING YOUR RESULTS

For each schema:

- **32-48 points:** Very strong schema—this is a major pattern in your life

- **24-31 points:** Strong schema—this significantly affects you

- **16-23 points:** Moderate schema—present but not dominant

- **8-15 points:** Mild or not present

What to do with your results:

1. **Identify your top 3-5 schemas** (highest scores). These are your primary targets for healing work.

2. **Notice which domains** have the most schemas. If you scored high on multiple schemas in one domain, that suggests a particular area of unmet needs.

3. **Don't panic if you score high on many schemas.** Most people have several. This just means you have work to do, which you're already doing by reading this book.

4. **Retake this assessment every 6 months** to track your progress. Scores should gradually decrease as you heal.

5. **Share your results with a therapist** if you're working with one. This gives them a roadmap for your work together.

Sample Profile:

Let's say someone scored:

- Abandonment: 42 (very strong)
- Defectiveness: 38 (very strong)
- Self-Sacrifice: 29 (strong)
- Failure: 26 (strong)
- Emotional Deprivation: 22 (moderate)

This person's healing work should focus primarily on abandonment and defectiveness schemas, with attention to self-sacrifice and failure. The emotional deprivation is connected but less intense.

Appendix B: Schema Mode Inventory

This inventory helps you identify which modes you experience and how often. Understanding your mode patterns helps you recognize when you're shifting between states.

Rating Scale: 1 = Never or almost never 2 = Rarely 3 = Sometimes 4 = Often 5 = Most of the time

Think about the past month when answering these questions.

CHILD MODES

Vulnerable Child Mode

_____ 1. I feel lonely, even when I'm around people. _____ 2. I feel small, scared, or helpless. _____ 3. I feel abandoned or rejected. _____ 4. I feel worthless, unloved, or unlovable. _____ 5. I feel overwhelmed and unable to cope. _____ 6. I feel needy and desperate for comfort. _____ 7. I feel sad, hurt, or on the verge of tears. _____ 8. I feel like a frightened child.

Total Score: _____ (32-40 = You spend significant time in Vulnerable Child mode)

Angry Child Mode

_____ 1. I feel intensely angry or enraged. _____ 2. I have explosive outbursts over small things. _____ 3. I feel furious when my needs aren't met. _____ 4. I want to yell, scream, or throw things. _____ 5. I feel so angry I can't control it. _____ 6. I feel like having a tantrum. _____ 7. I feel impatient and frustrated. _____ 8. My anger feels disproportionate to what triggered it.

Total Score: _____

Impulsive/Undisciplined Child Mode

____ 1. I act on impulses without thinking about consequences. ____ 2. I do whatever I feel like doing in the moment. ____ 3. I can't resist immediate gratification. ____ 4. I have trouble finishing tasks that bore me. ____ 5. I break rules or commitments when I feel like it. ____ 6. I get restless and need constant stimulation. ____ 7. I act selfishly without considering others. ____ 8. I give up easily when things get difficult.

Total Score: ____

Happy Child Mode

____ 1. I feel joyful, playful, and spontaneous. ____ 2. I feel safe, loved, and content. ____ 3. I feel connected to others in a positive way. ____ 4. I enjoy activities without worrying about performance. ____ 5. I feel optimistic about life. ____ 6. I can be silly and carefree. ____ 7. I feel at peace and satisfied. ____ 8. I feel like myself—authentic and free.

Total Score: ____ (Low scores here suggest you need to work on accessing Happy Child)

DYSFUNCTIONAL COPING MODES

Compliant Surrenderer Mode

____ 1. I go along with others even when I disagree. ____ 2. I act passive and submissive with others. ____ 3. I let people treat me poorly without defending myself. ____ 4. I apologize constantly, even when things aren't my fault. ____ 5. I suppress my feelings and needs to avoid conflict. ____ 6. I seek reassurance and approval excessively. ____ 7. I accept mistreatment as if I deserve it. ____ 8. I give in to others to keep the peace.

Total Score: ____

Detached Protector Mode

_____ 1. I feel emotionally numb or empty. _____ 2. I shut down and disconnect from my feelings. _____ 3. I zone out or feel foggy when stressed. _____ 4. I isolate myself from others. _____ 5. I feel like I'm just going through the motions of life. _____ 6. I avoid situations that might trigger emotions. _____ 7. I feel robotic or disconnected from myself. _____ 8. I use substances, activities, or distractions to avoid feeling.

Total Score: _____

Overcompensator Mode

_____ 1. I act aggressively or dominantly to stay in control. _____ 2. I push myself relentlessly to prove I'm good enough. _____ 3. I try to control situations and people around me. _____ 4. I act superior or dismiss others. _____ 5. I do the opposite of what my schemas predict to fight them. _____ 6. I appear confident on the outside but feel scared inside. _____ 7. I manipulate situations to get what I want. _____ 8. I can't show vulnerability or weakness.

Total Score: _____

DYSFUNCTIONAL PARENT MODES

Punitive Parent Mode

_____ 1. I attack myself with harsh criticism. _____ 2. I tell myself I'm worthless, stupid, or bad. _____ 3. I believe I deserve to be punished. _____ 4. I punish myself (through self-denial, self-harm, or harsh self-talk). _____ 5. I feel like I should suffer for my mistakes. _____ 6. I'm extremely unforgiving toward myself. _____ 7. I feel intense guilt and shame over normal imperfections. _____ 8. I have a cruel inner voice that tears me down.

Total Score: ____

Demanding Parent Mode

____ 1. I pressure myself constantly to do more and be better. ____ 2. I feel like nothing I do is ever good enough. ____ 3. I push myself to meet impossibly high standards. ____ 4. I feel guilty when I rest or relax. ____ 5. I focus on productivity and achievement constantly. ____ 6. I compare myself to others and feel I should be doing more. ____ 7. I can't enjoy accomplishments—I immediately focus on the next goal. ____ 8. I tell myself I "should" or "must" do things.

Total Score: ____

HEALTHY ADULT MODE

____ 1. I make balanced decisions considering both logic and feelings. ____ 2. I handle responsibilities without being driven or perfectionistic. ____ 3. I set appropriate boundaries with others. ____ 4. I comfort myself when I'm upset. ____ 5. I stand up to my inner critic with self-compassion. ____ 6. I can ask for what I need clearly and directly. ____ 7. I solve problems calmly and rationally. ____ 8. I balance taking care of myself with caring for others. ____ 9. I can tolerate uncomfortable emotions without acting impulsively. ____ 10. I feel like a competent adult handling life.

Total Score: ____ (40-50 = Strong Healthy Adult; 30-39 = Developing Healthy Adult; Below 30 = Needs significant work)

INTERPRETING YOUR MODE RESULTS

Look for patterns:

1. Which mode do you score highest in? This is your "go-to" mode under stress. For example:

- High Detached Protector = You shut down emotionally

- High Compliant Surrenderer = You give in and accept poor treatment

- High Overcompensator = You fight and control to protect yourself

2. What's your mode sequence? Many people have a predictable pattern:

- Vulnerable Child → Punitive Parent → Detached Protector

- Vulnerable Child → Angry Child → Overcompensator

- Vulnerable Child → Compliant Surrenderer

Understanding your sequence helps you interrupt it.

3. How strong is your Healthy Adult? If your Healthy Adult score is low (below 30), that's your primary focus. You need to build this mode before you can manage the others effectively.

4. How accessible is your Happy Child? If your Happy Child score is very low (below 15), you've lost touch with joy and spontaneity. This is a sign that schema work has cut you off from positive emotions.

Mode Profile Example:

Someone scores:

- Vulnerable Child: 31 (high)

- Punitive Parent: 36 (very high)

- Detached Protector: 28 (high)

- Healthy Adult: 22 (low)

- Happy Child: 11 (very low)

Interpretation: This person frequently feels vulnerable and scared. Their Punitive Parent immediately attacks them when they feel vulnerable, which is extremely painful. To escape the pain, they shut down into Detached Protector mode. Their Healthy Adult is weak and can't protect them from the Punitive Parent. They've completely lost touch with joy and play.

Healing priorities:

1. Build Healthy Adult mode

2. Combat Punitive Parent mode

3. Comfort Vulnerable Child mode

4. Gradually reconnect with Happy Child mode

Your Mode Tracking Exercise

For the next week, track which modes you experience each day:

Day 1: Morning mode: _____ Afternoon mode: _____ Evening mode: _____ What triggered mode shifts? _____

Do this for a full week. You'll start seeing patterns about:

- What time of day you're in which mode

- What situations trigger mode shifts

- How long you stay in each mode

- How easily you can access Healthy Adult

This awareness is the first step to changing mode patterns.

Appendix C: Daily Schema Journal Template

Keeping a schema journal helps you track patterns, recognize triggers, and monitor your progress. Here are several journal templates you can use.

TEMPLATE 1: BASIC SCHEMA TRIGGER LOG

Use this daily to track when schemas get activated.

Date: _____

Situation/Trigger: What happened? Where were you? Who was involved?

Schema Activated: Which schema got triggered? (abandonment, defectiveness, failure, etc.)

Thoughts: What went through your mind?

Feelings: What emotions did you experience? How intense (1-10)?

Body Sensations: What did you notice in your body? (tight chest, tense shoulders, nausea, etc.)

Behavior: What did you do? How did you react?

Mode(s): Which mode(s) were you in? (Vulnerable Child, Punitive Parent, etc.)

Coping Style: Did you surrender, avoid, or overcompensate?

Outcome: What happened? How long did it last?

What Would Healthy Adult Say? Looking back, what would a compassionate, rational response be?

TEMPLATE 2: SCHEMA CHALLENGE LOG

Use this when you want to challenge schema-driven thoughts.

Date: _____

Schema-Driven Thought: What is the schema telling you?

Which Schema:

Evidence For This Thought: What makes this seem true?

1. _____

2. _____

3. _____

Evidence Against This Thought: What contradicts this belief?

1. _____

2. _____

3. _____

Alternative Explanation: What's a more balanced way to see this situation?

_____

_____

Healthy Adult Response: What would you tell a friend in this situation?

_____

_____

How True Does the Schema Feel Now? (1-10) Before: _____ After: _____

_____

TEMPLATE 3: MODE SHIFT TRACKER

Use this to track how you move between modes during the day.

Date: _____

Time	Mode	What Triggered It	How Long It Lasted	How I Shifted Out
8am	Healthy Adult	Woke up refreshed	2 hours	Boss criticism
10am	Vulnerable Child	Boss email	30 min	Called friend
10:30am	Punitive Parent	Self-attacking	1 hour	Used flash cards

Patterns I Notice:

_____

_____

What Helped Me Access Healthy Adult:

_____

What I Want to Try Tomorrow:

_____

_____

TEMPLATE 4: WEEKLY SCHEMA REVIEW

Use this once a week to see larger patterns.

Week of: _____

Most Active Schemas This Week:

1. _____

2. _____

3. _____

Most Common Triggers:

_____

_____

Most Frequent Mode Pattern:

_____

Times I Caught Myself Early:

_____

_____

Times I Responded from Healthy Adult:

Times I Got Stuck in Old Patterns:

What I Learned:

What I Want to Work On Next Week:

Progress I Notice: (Even small things count!)

TEMPLATE 5: EXPERIENTIAL WORK LOG

Use this after doing imagery rescripting or other experiential exercises.

Date: _____

Exercise I Did: (Imagery rescripting, empty chair, etc.)

Schema/Mode Targeted:

Memory or Situation I Worked With:

_____

_____

What Came Up: (Emotions, insights, memories)

_____

_____

What the Child Part Needed:

_____

What I (as Healthy Adult) Provided:

_____

New Understanding or Insight:

_____

_____

How I Feel After This Work:

_____

How This Relates to Current Patterns:

_____

What I Want to Remember:

_____

_____

TEMPLATE 6: BEHAVIORAL EXPERIMENT LOG

Use this when you're trying new behaviors to challenge schemas.

Date: _____

Schema I'm Challenging:

_____

Old Behavior (Schema-Driven): What I usually do in this situation

---

New Behavior (Healthy Adult): What I'm going to try instead

Schema Prediction: What does my schema say will happen if I try the new behavior?

What Actually Happened:

How	It	Felt:	Before:
_____			During:
_____			After:
_____			

What This Taught Me:

Will I Try This Again?

TEMPLATE 7: MONTHLY PROGRESS REVIEW

Use this once a month to track overall healing.

Month: _____

Schemas Worked On:

Progress This Month: (Changes in thoughts, feelings, behaviors)

_____

_____

_____

Challenges This Month:

_____

_____

Setbacks and What I Learned:

_____

_____

Healthy Adult Moments: Times I responded well

_____

_____

Happy Child Moments: Times I experienced joy, play, spontaneity

_____

Support I Received:

_____

Tools That Helped Most:

_____

Goals for Next Month:

_____

_____

How I'll Celebrate Progress:

_____

JOURNALING TIPS

1. Consistency matters more than length. Better to write three sentences daily than three pages once a month.

2. Write soon after events. Details fade quickly. Journal within a few hours if possible.

3. Be honest. This is for you. No one else needs to see it.

4. Notice patterns. Review your journals weekly to spot recurring triggers and responses.

5. Celebrate small wins. Note every time you caught yourself, every Healthy Adult response, every moment of progress.

6. Don't judge your entries. You're documenting a process, not performing for an audience.

7. Use what works. Some people prefer detailed writing, others bullet points. Some use apps, others paper. Find your style.

Appendix D: Finding a Schema Therapist

Schema therapy is a specialized approach. Not every therapist is trained in it. Here's how to find a qualified schema therapist and what to look for.

WHERE TO FIND SCHEMA THERAPISTS

1. International Society of Schema Therapy (ISST)

Website: www.schematherapysociety.org

The ISST is the official organization for schema therapy. Their website has a therapist directory where you can search by location.

Search Features:

- Filter by country, state/province, city

- Filter by specialty (individual therapy, couples, children, etc.)

- See therapist's certification level

Certification Levels:

- **Certified Schema Therapist:** Completed full training, passed exams, demonstrated competence

- **Advanced Certified Schema Therapist:** Additional training and supervision

- **Supervisor/Trainer:** Can train other therapists

Higher certification generally means more expertise, but newer therapists can still be excellent.

2. Psychology Today Therapist Directory

Website: www.psychologytoday.com/us/therapists

How to Search:

1. Enter your location
2. Under "Types of Therapy," select "Schema Therapy"
3. Review profiles of therapists who appear

What to Look For:

- "Schema Therapy" listed in their specialties
- Training from ISST or schema therapy institutes
- Experience with your specific schemas/issues

3. Local University Counseling Psychology Programs

Many universities with clinical psychology programs have:

- Training clinics where advanced students practice schema therapy under supervision (often lower cost)
- Faculty who practice schema therapy
- Referral lists of schema therapists in the area

Call the psychology department and ask: "Do you have any faculty or supervised students who practice schema therapy?"

4. Professional Referral Networks

American Psychological Association (APA): www.apa.org/helpcenter **Association for Behavioral and Cognitive Therapies (ABCT):** www.abct.org

Call or use their online directories to find cognitive-behavioral therapists, then ask if they're trained in schema therapy.

5. Personal Referrals

Ask:

- Your current therapist (if you have one)
- Your doctor

- Friends who've been in therapy
- Online support groups focused on schema therapy

WHAT TO ASK POTENTIAL THERAPISTS

When you contact a schema therapist, ask these questions:

Training and Experience:

1. "Are you trained in schema therapy? Where did you receive your training?"

2. "Are you certified by the International Society of Schema Therapy?"

3. "How long have you been practicing schema therapy?"

4. "What percentage of your practice is schema therapy?"

5. "Have you worked with [your specific schemas/issues]?"

Approach:

1. "How do you typically structure schema therapy?"

2. "Do you use experiential techniques like imagery rescripting?"

3. "How active or directive are you as a therapist?"

4. "Do you integrate other approaches with schema therapy?"

Practical Matters:

1. "What are your fees?"

2. "Do you take my insurance?"

3. "How long are sessions?" (Standard is 45-50 minutes, but some schema therapists do longer sessions)

4. "What's your cancellation policy?"

5. "How often would we meet?" (Weekly is typical)

6. "Do you offer video sessions?"

Compatibility:

1. "Have you worked with clients like me before?" (Your age, background, issues)

2. "What's your style?" (Warm? Challenging? Structured? Flexible?)

3. "Can we do a consultation session to see if we're a good fit?"

RED FLAGS - When to Keep Looking

Avoid therapists who:

- Claim they can cure you quickly (schema therapy takes time)

- Seem judgmental or critical during initial contact

- Won't answer questions about their training

- Promise specific outcomes

- Pressure you to commit immediately

- Don't maintain professional boundaries

- Make you feel uncomfortable or unsafe

- Are dismissive of your concerns

- Don't seem to understand schema therapy concepts when you ask

Trust your gut. If something feels off in the first session, it's okay to try someone else.

WHAT TO EXPECT IN SCHEMA THERAPY

First Sessions (1-3):

- Assessment of your schemas
- Discussion of your history and current problems
- Explanation of how schema therapy works
- Goal setting
- Building rapport

Early Phase (Months 1-6):

- Identifying schemas and modes
- Connecting current problems to past experiences
- Learning concepts and tools
- Beginning cognitive work
- Building Healthy Adult mode

Middle Phase (Months 6-18):

- Deeper experiential work
- Imagery rescripting
- Processing emotional memories
- Behavioral experiments
- Challenging schemas actively

Later Phase (Months 18+):

- Consolidating gains
- Applying skills to life
- Reducing session frequency
- Planning for maintenance
- Eventual termination

Total Duration: Most people need 1-3 years for significant schema healing, though some feel better sooner.

COST AND INSURANCE

Typical Costs:

- **With insurance:** Copay only ($0-$50 per session)
- **Without insurance:** $100-$300+ per session depending on location and therapist experience

Insurance Tips:

1. Call your insurance company: "Do you cover outpatient psychotherapy?"
2. Ask: "Do I need a referral? Is there a limit on sessions?"
3. Get a list of in-network providers
4. Call therapists on that list and ask if they practice schema therapy

If Schema Therapists Aren't Covered:

- Ask about sliding scale fees (reduced rates based on income)
- Consider seeing someone less frequently (every 2 weeks instead of weekly)
- Look for training clinics (lower cost)
- Save one main issue for a monthly schema therapy session while doing weekly therapy with a less expensive generalist

---

ALTERNATIVES IF YOU CAN'T FIND A SCHEMA THERAPIST

Option 1: Regular CBT Therapist with Schema Focus

Find a cognitive-behavioral therapist and ask: "I'd like to focus on core beliefs from childhood. Can we work on that using schema therapy principles?"

Many CBT therapists know some schema therapy even if it's not their main approach.

Option 2: Self-Directed Work with Check-Ins

Use this book and other schema therapy resources for self-directed work. Meet with a general therapist monthly to process what comes up and stay on track.

Option 3: Online Schema Therapy

Some schema therapists offer video sessions to clients in other states/countries. Search for "schema therapy telehealth" or "schema therapy online."

Option 4: Schema Therapy Groups

Some therapists run schema therapy groups. This can be more affordable and provides peer support. Ask local therapists if they know of any groups.

Option 5: Intensive Programs

Some treatment centers offer week-long or month-long intensive schema therapy programs. This is expensive but efficient.

EVALUATING IF IT'S WORKING

After 3 months, you should notice:

- Better understanding of your patterns
- Slightly less intense reactions to triggers
- More ability to catch yourself mid-pattern
- Beginning to access Healthy Adult mode

After 6 months:

- Clear reduction in schema activation frequency
- Faster recovery from triggers
- Changing some behaviors
- Feeling more in control

After 1 year:

- Significant improvement in targeted schemas
- Much stronger Healthy Adult mode
- New behaviors becoming more natural
- Better relationships

If you're not seeing any progress after 6 months:

- Discuss this with your therapist
- You might need a different approach or different therapist
- You might need to address trauma more directly first
- You might need medication in addition to therapy

ONLINE RESOURCES AND SUPPORT

Schema Therapy Institute (New York): www.schematherapy.com

- Articles, videos, resources
- Training information

Schema Therapy Training (Multiple Locations): Various institutes worldwide offer training for therapists, but their websites often have free resources for clients.

Online Support Groups:

- Reddit: r/SchemaTherapy

- Facebook: Search "Schema Therapy Support"
- Online forums dedicated to schema therapy

YouTube: Search "schema therapy" for educational videos, lectures, and demonstrations.

QUESTIONS ABOUT THERAPY

Q: How do I know if a therapist is right for me? You should feel heard, respected, and safe. You don't have to like everything they say, but you should feel they're on your side. Trust your instincts.

Q: What if I can't afford therapy? Look for community mental health centers, training clinics, sliding scale options, or online resources for self-directed work. Something is better than nothing.

Q: Can I do schema therapy without a therapist? You can do significant work on your own using books, workbooks, and online resources. A therapist helps, especially with deeper experiential work, but it's not absolutely required.

Q: How often should I see a therapist? Weekly is standard. Some people do twice weekly for intensive work. Less than weekly makes progress slower but can still work.

Q: What if my therapist doesn't know about schemas but I can't find one who does? Bring this book to therapy. Say, "I've been reading about schema therapy and I think it fits my problems. Can we work on these concepts together?" Many good therapists will learn alongside you.

Appendix E: Recommended Reading and Resources

Here are carefully selected resources to deepen your understanding of schema therapy and related topics.

ESSENTIAL SCHEMA THERAPY BOOKS

For General Readers:

1. "Reinventing Your Life" by Jeffrey Young and Janet Klosko

- The original self-help book on schema therapy

- Written for general audiences

- Covers all 18 schemas with examples

- Includes practical exercises

- Best starting point after this book

2. "Schema Therapy: A Practitioner's Guide" by Jeffrey Young, Janet Klosko, and Marjorie Weishaar

- More technical than "Reinventing Your Life"

- Written for therapists but valuable for motivated clients

- Comprehensive coverage of theory and techniques

- Includes case studies

3. "Breaking Negative Thinking Patterns" by Gitta Jacob

- Focuses on schema modes

- Very accessible language

- Excellent for understanding mode work

- Includes exercises and worksheets

4. "The Schema Therapy Clinician's Guide" by Joan Farrell and Ida Shaw

- Practical and clear
- Good for understanding how therapy actually works
- Includes protocols for different problems

WORKBOOKS FOR SELF-DIRECTED PRACTICE

1. "The Schema Therapy Patient's Handbook" by Dianne Farrell

- Practical exercises you can do at home
- Worksheets for identifying schemas and modes
- Step-by-step guidance

2. "Schema Therapy Distinctive Features" by Eshkol Rafaeli, David Bernstein, and Jeffrey Young

- Short, clear explanations of key concepts
- Good reference guide
- Organized in bite-sized sections

RELATED BOOKS ON CHILDHOOD WOUNDS

1. "The Body Keeps the Score" by Bessel van der Kolk

- About how trauma affects the body and brain
- Explains why schemas are so hard to change
- Discusses healing approaches
- Groundbreaking and accessible

2. "Complex PTSD: From Surviving to Thriving" by Pete Walker

- For people with childhood trauma

- Covers "emotional flashbacks" (similar to schema activation)
- Practical coping strategies
- Compassionate tone

3. "Running on Empty" by Jonice Webb

- About emotional neglect and emotional deprivation
- Helps you understand what you didn't get as a child
- Includes exercises for healing
- Very validating

4. "Adult Children of Emotionally Immature Parents" by Lindsay Gibson

- Explains how immature parents create schemas
- Helps you understand your parents without excusing them
- Strategies for current relationships with family

BOOKS ON SELF-COMPASSION

1. "Self-Compassion" by Kristin Neff

- Essential for combating Punitive Parent mode
- Research-based but accessible
- Practical exercises
- Audio guided meditations available

2. "The Mindful Self-Compassion Workbook" by Kristin Neff and Christopher Germer

- Structured program for building self-compassion
- Particularly helpful for harsh self-criticism
- Includes recorded meditations

BOOKS ON ATTACHMENT

1. "Attached" by Amir Levine and Rachel Heller

- About attachment styles in adult relationships
- Very readable
- Helps you understand relationship patterns
- Directly related to abandonment and enmeshment schemas

2. "Wired for Love" by Stan Tatkin

- How attachment affects romantic relationships
- Neuroscience-based but accessible
- Practical advice for couples

ONLINE COURSES AND VIDEOS

Schema Therapy Institute YouTube Channel

- Free lectures and demonstrations
- Watch Dr. Young explain concepts
- See schema therapy techniques in action

Udemy and Coursera

- Occasionally offer courses on schema therapy
- Look for courses on cognitive-behavioral therapy and attachment theory

TED Talks

- Search for talks on self-compassion, childhood trauma, and emotional wounds
- Kristin Neff's TED talk on self-compassion is excellent

APPS AND DIGITAL TOOLS

For Tracking Moods and Schemas:

- **Daylio:** Mood tracking with notes

- **Moodpath:** Depression and anxiety tracking

- **Bearable:** Comprehensive mood and trigger tracking

For Meditation and Self-Compassion:

- **Insight Timer:** Free meditations, including self-compassion practices

- **Calm:** Guided meditations and sleep stories

- **Headspace:** Structured meditation programs

For Journaling:

- **Day One:** Digital journaling app

- **Journey:** Cross-platform journaling

- **Penzu:** Private online journal

WEBSITES AND ONLINE RESOURCES

www.schematherapysociety.org

- Official schema therapy organization

- Therapist directory

- Research articles

- Conference information

www.schematherapy.com

- Schema Therapy Institute

- Articles and resources
- Assessment tools

www.psychologytools.com

- Free worksheets and handouts
- Schema therapy resources
- Evidence-based information

www.getselfhelp.co.uk

- Free CBT and schema therapy resources
- Printable worksheets
- Audio files

PODCASTS

"The Therapist Uncensored"

- Covers attachment theory extensively
- Relevant to understanding schema development
- Accessible and engaging

"The One You Feed"

- About personal growth and healing
- Many episodes relevant to schema work

"Speaking of Psychology" (American Psychological Association)

- Various topics including trauma and attachment
- Evidence-based content

ACADEMIC RESOURCES

(For those who want to dive deep)

Key Research Articles:

1. Giesen-Bloo et al. (2006). "Outpatient Psychotherapy for Borderline Personality Disorder: Randomized Trial of Schema-Focused Therapy vs Transference-Focused Psychotherapy"

- Landmark study showing schema therapy's effectiveness

2. Farrell, Shaw, & Webber (2009). "A Schema-Focused Approach to Group Psychotherapy"

- About group schema therapy

Where to Find Research:

- Google Scholar (scholar.google.com)
- PubMed (pubmed.ncbi.nlm.nih.gov)
- Search: "schema therapy outcomes" or "schema therapy effectiveness"

SUPPORT COMMUNITIES

Reddit:

- r/SchemaTherapy: Questions, discussions, support
- r/CPTSD: For complex trauma (overlaps with schema therapy)
- r/attachment_theory: About attachment patterns

Facebook Groups:

- Search "Schema Therapy Support Group"
- Search "Schema Therapy Healing"
- Private groups for specific schemas

RESOURCES FOR SPECIFIC ISSUES

For Abandonment Issues:

- "Insecure in Love" by Leslie Becker-Phelps
- "The Fear of Abandonment Workbook" by Michelle Skeen

For Perfectionism (Unrelenting Standards):

- "The Gifts of Imperfection" by Brené Brown
- "When Perfect Isn't Good Enough" by Martin Antony and Richard Swinson

For People-Pleasing (Self-Sacrifice):

- "The Disease to Please" by Harriet Braiker
- "Set Boundaries, Find Peace" by Nedra Tawwab

For Shame (Defectiveness):

- "Healing the Shame That Binds You" by John Bradshaw
- "I Thought It Was Just Me" by Brené Brown

For Childhood Trauma:

- "The Courage to Heal" by Ellen Bass and Laura Davis
- "Healing Your Emotional Self" by Beverly Engel

FOR PARENTS

To Avoid Passing Schemas to Children:

"Parenting from the Inside Out" by Daniel Siegel and Mary Hartzell

- How your history affects your parenting
- Breaking intergenerational patterns

"The Whole-Brain Child" by Daniel Siegel and Tina Payne Bryson

- Child development and emotional intelligence
- Practical parenting strategies

"How to Talk So Kids Will Listen..." by Adele Faber and Elaine Mazlish

- Communication that validates children
- Prevents development of schemas

CREATING YOUR PERSONAL RESOURCE LIBRARY

Suggested Starting Point:

Month 1-3:

- Read this book ("Schema Therapy for Beginners")
- Add: "Reinventing Your Life" by Young and Klosko
- Subscribe to one schema therapy podcast

Month 4-6:

- Add: One book specific to your main schema
- Join one online support community
- Start using a mood tracking app

Month 6-12:

- Add: "The Body Keeps the Score" by van der Kolk
- Add: "Self-Compassion" by Kristin Neff
- Consider starting therapy if you haven't already

Year 2+:

- Dive into more specialized resources

- Explore related topics (attachment, trauma, mindfulness)
- Consider training in schema therapy techniques yourself

WARNING ABOUT ONLINE INFORMATION

Be careful with:

- Unverified social media advice
- People claiming to cure schemas quickly
- Expensive "miracle" programs
- Unqualified "coaches" claiming expertise
- Information that contradicts evidence-based research

Stick to:

- Resources from qualified professionals
- Books by recognized experts
- Official schema therapy organizations
- Evidence-based approaches
- Recommendations from your therapist

Glossary of Schema Therapy Terms

A

Adaptive Schema A healthy, functional belief about yourself and the world that helps you meet your needs effectively. Example: "I'm worthy of love" or "I can handle challenges."

Angry Child Mode A child mode characterized by intense anger, rage, or frustration that arises when the Vulnerable Child's needs have been repeatedly ignored or violated.

Avoidance (Coping Style) A way of dealing with schemas by staying away from situations, people, or feelings that might activate the schema. Can include emotional numbing, substance use, or isolation.

B

Behavioral Experiments Structured activities where you test schema-driven predictions by trying new behaviors and observing what actually happens. Used to challenge schemas with real-world evidence.

C

Child Modes Emotional states that represent feelings and perspectives from childhood. Include Vulnerable Child, Angry Child, Impulsive/Undisciplined Child, and Happy Child.

Cognitive Techniques Methods that work with thoughts and beliefs to identify, challenge, and change schema-driven thinking patterns.

Compliant Surrenderer Mode A coping mode where you passively give in to your schemas and accept poor treatment without defending yourself.

Core Emotional Needs Universal human needs that, when unmet in childhood, lead to schema development. Include secure attachments, autonomy, freedom to express feelings, spontaneity/play, and realistic limits.

Coping Modes Ways of managing the pain of schemas. Include Compliant Surrenderer, Detached Protector, and Overcompensator modes.

Coping Styles The three main strategies for dealing with schemas: surrender (accepting the schema as true), avoidance (staying away from schema triggers), and overcompensation (doing the opposite of what the schema predicts).

D

Defectiveness/Shame Schema The belief that you are fundamentally flawed, bad, or unworthy of love, and that if people really knew you, they would reject you.

Demanding Parent Mode An internalized critical voice that pushes you to achieve more, be better, work harder, and meet impossibly high standards.

Detached Protector Mode A coping mode where you emotionally shut down, feel numb, and disconnect from feelings to avoid schema pain.

Dysfunctional Parent Modes Internalized critical voices from childhood authority figures. Include Punitive Parent and Demanding Parent modes.

E

Early Maladaptive Schema (EMS) A broad, pervasive pattern of thoughts, emotions, memories, and body sensations about yourself and relationships that developed in childhood and causes problems in adult life.

Emotional Deprivation Schema The belief that your emotional needs for nurturance, empathy, or protection will never be adequately met by others.

Emotional Inhibition Schema The belief that you must control or suppress your emotions because showing feelings is dangerous, embarrassing, or unacceptable.

Empathic Confrontation A therapeutic technique where problematic patterns are addressed with both compassion for the pain underneath and firm acknowledgment of self-destructive consequences.

Empty Chair Dialogue An experiential technique where you have conversations with imagined people (or parts of yourself) sitting in empty chairs to express emotions and gain new perspectives.

Enmeshment/Undeveloped Self Schema The belief that you cannot function or survive without being extremely close to someone else, with no clear sense of your own identity.

Entitlement/Grandiosity Schema The belief that you are special, deserve special treatment, and that normal rules don't apply to you.

Experiential Techniques Methods that work with emotions and memories, including imagery rescripting, empty chair work, and limited reparenting, to create emotional healing.

F

Failure Schema The belief that you are inadequate, will fail at anything important, and are less capable than others.

Flash Cards Cards with schema-challenging messages that you read regularly to reinforce Healthy Adult perspectives.

G

Graded Exposure A behavioral technique where you gradually face feared situations in a hierarchy from least to most challenging.

H

Happy Child Mode A healthy child mode characterized by feeling joyful, playful, spontaneous, safe, loved, and content.

Healthy Adult Mode The integrated, balanced, functional part of you that can make good decisions, nurture your child modes, combat dysfunctional parent modes, and handle life's challenges effectively.

Historical Role-Play A cognitive technique where you have a conversation between your current adult self and your child self to gain new perspective on past events.

I

Imagery Rescripting A powerful experiential technique where you revisit painful childhood memories in imagination and change them by having your adult self enter the scene and provide what the child needed.

Impulsive/Undisciplined Child Mode A child mode characterized by acting on impulses without thinking about consequences, difficulty with self-discipline, and low frustration tolerance.

Insufficient Self-Control/Self-Discipline Schema The belief that you cannot control your impulses or make yourself do things that are difficult or boring.

L

Limited Reparenting A therapeutic approach where the therapist provides some of what the client needed but didn't receive in childhood—validation, acceptance, guidance—within appropriate professional boundaries.

M

Mistrust/Abuse Schema The belief that others will hurt, abuse, manipulate, or take advantage of you.

Mode A temporary emotional state that combines schemas, coping styles, and emotional responses active at a particular moment. People shift between modes throughout the day.

N

Negativity/Pessimism Schema The belief that bad things will happen, life won't work out, and it's pointless to focus on positive aspects.

O

Overcompensation (Coping Style) A way of dealing with schemas by doing the opposite of what the schema predicts, often rigidly or extremely. Fighting against the schema rather than accepting or avoiding it.

Overcompensator Mode A coping mode where you try to fight schemas through aggressive, controlling, or perfectionistic behavior that appears strong but is actually protective.

P

Parent Modes See Dysfunctional Parent Modes.

Punitiveness Schema The belief that people (including yourself) should be harshly punished for mistakes, with little room for forgiveness or understanding.

Punitive Parent Mode An internalized harsh, critical voice that attacks you for mistakes, feelings, or needs, telling you that you deserve punishment or are worthless.

S

Schema See Early Maladaptive Schema.

Schema Activation When a situation triggers a schema, causing the associated thoughts, emotions, and body sensations to arise.

Schema Domain A category grouping related schemas based on similar unmet needs. The five domains are: Disconnection and Rejection, Impaired Autonomy and Performance, Impaired Limits, Other-Directedness, and Overvigilance and Inhibition.

Schema Maintenance Ways that schemas perpetuate themselves, including selective attention to confirming evidence and behaviors that create self-fulfilling prophecies.

Schema Mode See Mode.

Schema Therapy An integrative psychotherapy approach developed by Jeffrey Young that addresses deep-rooted patterns from childhood by combining cognitive, experiential, and behavioral techniques.

Self-Sacrifice Schema The belief that you must focus excessively on meeting others' needs at the expense of your own to avoid guilt or maintain relationships.

Social Isolation/Alienation Schema The belief that you are fundamentally different from others, don't belong, and will always be an outsider.

Subjugation Schema The belief that you must submit to others' control to avoid anger, retaliation, or abandonment, and that your own desires and feelings don't matter.

Surrender (Coping Style) A way of dealing with schemas by accepting them as true and behaving in ways that confirm them, essentially giving up on fighting or avoiding the schema.

T

Trigger A situation, person, or event that activates a schema, causing old patterns to emerge.

U

Unrelenting Standards/Hypercriticalness Schema The belief that you must meet extremely high standards, that good enough is never enough, and that achievement is more important than happiness.

Unmet Needs See Core Emotional Needs.

V

Vulnerable Child Mode A child mode characterized by feeling scared, hurt, abandoned, lonely, helpless, or unworthy—the emotional state of a child whose needs are not being met.

Vulnerability to Harm or Illness Schema The belief that catastrophe could strike at any moment and that you are not safe from medical, natural, criminal, or financial disasters.

Y

Young Schema Questionnaire (YSQ) A standardized assessment tool developed by Jeffrey Young to identify and measure the 18 early maladaptive schemas.

These appendices provide you with practical tools to apply schema therapy concepts to your life. Use the questionnaires to identify your patterns, the journal templates to track your progress, the therapist guidelines to find professional help, and the resources to continue learning. Remember: understanding your schemas is just the beginning. The real work happens when you apply these tools consistently over time. Keep going. You're worth the effort.

References

Arntz, A., & Jacob, G. (2013). Schema therapy in practice: An introductory guide to the schema mode approach. *International Journal of Cognitive Therapy, 6*(2), 185-207.

Bach, B., Lockwood, G., & Young, J. E. (2018). A new look at the schema therapy model: Organization and role of early maladaptive schemas. *Cognitive Behaviour Therapy, 47*(4), 328-349.

Bamelis, L. L., Evers, S. M., Spinhoven, P., & Arntz, A. (2014). Results of a multicenter randomized controlled trial of the clinical effectiveness of schema therapy for personality disorders. *American Journal of Psychiatry, 171*(3), 305-322.

Bowlby, J. (1988). A secure base: Parent-child attachment and healthy human development. *Basic Books.*

Farrell, J. M., Shaw, I. A., & Webber, M. A. (2009). A schema-focused approach to group psychotherapy for outpatients with borderline personality disorder: A randomized controlled trial. *Journal of Behavior Therapy and Experimental Psychiatry, 40*(2), 317-328.

Giesen-Bloo, J., van Dyck, R., Spinhoven, P., van Tilburg, W., Dirksen, C., van Asselt, T., Kremers, I., Nadort, M., & Arntz, A. (2006). Outpatient psychotherapy for borderline personality disorder: Randomized trial of schema-focused therapy vs transference-focused psychotherapy. *Archives of General Psychiatry, 63*(6), 649-658.

Hawke, L. D., Provencher, M. D., & Arntz, A. (2011). Early maladaptive schemas in the risk for bipolar spectrum disorders. *Journal of Affective Disorders, 133*(3), 428-436.

Jacob, G. A., & Arntz, A. (2013). Schema therapy for personality disorders: A review. *International Journal of Cognitive Therapy, 6*(2), 171-185.

Lobbestael, J., van Vreeswijk, M., & Arntz, A. (2007). Shedding light on schema modes: A clarification of the mode concept and its current research status. *Netherlands Journal of Psychology, 63*(3), 76-85.

Malogiannis, I. A., Arntz, A., Spyropoulou, A., Tsartsara, E., Aggeli, A., Karveli, S., Vlavianou, M., Pehlivanidis, A., Papadimitriou, G. N., & Zervas, I. (2014). Schema therapy for patients with chronic depression: A single case series study. *Journal of Behavior Therapy and Experimental Psychiatry, 45*(3), 319-329.

Nordahl, H. M., Holthe, H., & Haugum, J. A. (2005). Early maladaptive schemas in patients with or without personality disorders: Does schema modification predict symptomatic relief? *Clinical Psychology & Psychotherapy, 12*(2), 142-149.

Rafaeli, E., Bernstein, D. P., & Young, J. E. (2011). *Schema therapy: Distinctive features*. Routledge.

Renner, F., Lobbestael, J., Peeters, F., Arntz, A., & Huibers, M. (2012). Early maladaptive schemas in depressed patients: Stability and relation with depressive symptoms over the course of treatment. *Journal of Affective Disorders, 136*(3), 581-590.

Siegel, D. J. (2012). *The developing mind: How relationships and the brain interact to shape who we are* (2nd ed.). Guilford Press.

Thimm, J. C., & Chang, M. (2022). Early maladaptive schemas and mental disorders in adulthood: A systematic review and meta-analysis. *International Journal of Cognitive Therapy, 15*(3), 371-413.

van der Kolk, B. A. (2014). *The body keeps the score: Brain, mind, and body in the healing of trauma*. Viking.

Young, J. E. (1990). *Cognitive therapy for personality disorders: A schema-focused approach*. Professional Resource Press.

Young, J. E., & Brown, G. (2001). Young Schema Questionnaire: Special edition. *Cognitive Therapy Center of New York*.

Young, J. E., Klosko, J. S., & Weishaar, M. E. (2003). *Schema therapy: A practitioner's guide*. Guilford Press.

Zanarini, M. C., Frankenburg, F. R., Reich, D. B., & Fitzmaurice, G. (2012). Attainment and stability of sustained symptomatic remission and recovery among patients with borderline personality disorder and axis II comparison subjects: A 16-year prospective follow-up study. *American Journal of Psychiatry, 169*(5), 476-483.

www.ingramcontent.com/pod-product-compliance
Lightning Source LLC
Chambersburg PA
CBHW071434090426
42737CB00011B/1654